DIRTBAG RICH

Praise for *Dirtbag Rich*

"For everybody, young and not so young, who yearns to stop running the maze and start building a life that's more authentic, ecstatic, surprising, alive, Blake Boles is here to point the way. Blake has walked the walk, hiked the hike, and danced the dance. He offers counsel that's both practical and spiritual, in writing that's sharp, energetic, and heartfelt. Put this book in your backpack and hit the great wide road."

—WILLIAM DERESIEWICZ
New York Times bestselling author of *Excellent Sheep*

"*Dirtbag Rich* is refreshing, encouraging, and entirely thought-provoking. Taking a walk through Blake's out-of-the-box worldview makes me want to live my dirtbag-inspired life with greater intention, deeper presence, and a stronger sense of connection."

—JENNY ABEGG
Patagonia trail running ambassador and co-founder of Better Trail

"Many people—maybe even most people—would prefer to fail conventionally than defy social expectations in pursuit of deeper meaning. If you're one of the few looking to strike out for a life of greater authenticity and autonomy, Blake Boles's *Dirtbag Rich* will offer you warm encouragement and practical advice from a fellow traveler."

—DAVE WHITSON
Author of *Pilgrimage: A Medieval Cure for Modern Ills*

"In an age where many are priced out, burned out, and done playing the game, *Dirtbag Rich* reframes wealth as free time, movement, and meaning—and offers practical ways to live it. We need more books like this."

—SCOTT STILLMAN
Author of *Wilderness: The Gateway To The Soul*

(Praise Continued)

"As a semi-nomadic freelance writer, I've often felt alone in my total freedom. No more after reading *Dirtbag Rich*! Blake Boles examines and celebrates what it is to live a meaningful life through the experiences of wild professionals (including himself) who live outside societal norms, illuminating that while no two paths are alike, the 'dirtbag rich' are a far-flung cadre of maverick spirits marching to their own beat."

—MORGAN SJOGREN
Author of *Path of Light* and *Outlandish*

"We all say 'money doesn't buy happiness,' but it's hard to move our focus to anything else most days. In *Dirtbag Rich*, Blake brings a unique perspective and curiosity to the question of how we might live differently. He may not have all the answers, but knows who to ask to share their wisdom."

—BRENDAN LEONARD
Writer, illustrator, and creator of Semi-Rad.com

"These days, a 'life of quiet desperation' involves a pointless office job, overdrawn bank account, and two depressing weeks of paid vacation. *Dirtbag Rich* offers practical inspiration for the part-time crusader, showing how there are plenty of achievable ways to have the exact opposite: meaningful work, sufficient money, and plenty of time to wander in the woods."

—TIM MATHIS
Author of *The Dirtbag's Guide to Life*

DIRTBAG RICH

High Freedom, Low Income, Deep Purpose

Blake Boles

with illustrations by Brendan Leonard

Copyright © 2026 Blake Boles

ISBN: 978-0-9860119-9-3
Library of Congress Control Number: 2025923797

Cover design by Boja/99designs
Book design by Zoe Norvell

Published in Loon Lake, California, United States by Tells Peak Press.

Table of Contents

How Does One Survive This World? — 1

Introduction — 5

    No Glamour Here, Just Dirtbag Riches — 7
    What's A Dirtbag? — 9
    Dirtbagging Is Unsustainable, As Is Normal Life — 11
    The Cycle of Quitting Begins — 13
    A Love of Flight — 15
    A Different Way — 18
    About This Book — 21

The Right Party — 25

    This Is What I'm Supposed To Do? — 27
    Not My Kind Of Party — 28
    Fifteen Hours A Week — 29
    The Point Of Your Existence — 32
    You Really Don't Have To — 34

The Currency of Freedom — 39

    The Magic Trifecta — 41
    Build Your Own Escape Hatch — 44
    Be More Special — 47
    Lifestyles Of The Dirtbag Rich And Famous — 51

The Life-Changing Magic Of Being A Nature-Loving Tightwad — 55
Pay Less For Housing — 59
Get Creative With Human Services — 65
Choosing Time Over Money Is A Bloodsport — 70
How To Know If You're Wealthy — 74

A Dirtbag With A Cause — 79

What A Tingling Spine Says — 81
Slipperier Than A Catfish In A Vaseline Fight — 83
Ecstasy, Transcendence, And Adventure — 86
Gyrating Dirtbag Flower Children — 88
Drinking Fountains Of Meaning — 92
The Church Of The Wild — 94
A Diversified Relationship Portfolio — 98
Anti-Bullshit Jobs — 102
Freedom From And Freedom To — 105

"You Can't Do This Forever" — 111

Walking The Highline — 113
A Dirtbag Retirement Plan — 118
The Question Of Children — 121
Cool Aunts, Unconventional Educators, and Crazy Guys On Bikes — 123
Moderately Privileged And Highly Idealistic — 128
Nuts And Bolts — 131

Acknowledgments — 133

About the Author — 135

HOW DOES ONE SURVIVE THIS WORLD?

What do you do
when you're young, energetic, and full of potential,
priced out of the housing market,
disillusioned by world affairs,
and only feel whole
when moving your body swiftly through nature?

What do you do
when you don't want to play the same game as everyone else
but you also don't want to become a bum, nun, monk, or parasite
or end up dead in a bus in Alaska?

When most serious jobs feel morally suspect
When full-time work is a conveyor belt to burnout
When vacation allows only for recovery, not re-creation
Why contribute, why participate, why buy in?

Why listen to those who tell you to suck it up,
get serious, stop your griping, and take the damn job,
when they seem to inhabit a very different universe
and came of age in very different circumstances?

You try listening to the hustle bros
They're clever and enthusiastic
but still pray to the money gods

You follow the full-time athletes, artists, and explorers
They're beautiful and inspirational, with unfortunately little to say
about money, relationships, or finding work that supports such lives

You try the self-care: "I'm good enough, just as I am right now"
But "good enough" doesn't exempt you
from bills, debts, inflation, and social expectations

Older people call you talented and capable: "Don't waste your potential"
You wonder how much of this praise is genuine
And how much validates their own questionable choices

All you really know for sure:
You can put your faith in sunrises and sunsets
Sweat, dirt, and campfire smoke
Cold lakes and windy forests
Bird calls and rocky trails
One leg in front of another
And the rare souls who speak your same language

You don't need to become rich or famous
You just want to do good work, and not too much of it
and invest heavily in nature, relationships, and social causes

How does one do this
when anxious family, friends, and media
tell you to play it safe?

How does one participate in "capitalism"
without losing mind, body, soul
and still purchase a goose down sleeping bag?

How does one step away from the algorithm
of "work, nest, accumulate, reproduce, retire"
and still have warmth, friends, community, safety?

Who is asking these questions
and where are the answers?

How does one survive this world?

INTRODUCTION

NO GLAMOUR HERE—
JUST DIRTBAG RICHES

HI, I'M BLAKE.

I'm not wealthy or famous.

I don't have a house, car, spouse, child, advanced degree, or prestigious title.

I lack many things that others my age possess.

What I do have is my own little version of the good life: one overflowing with freedom, nature, travel, adventure, romance, and friendship.

For almost two decades now I've worked just a few months each year. The rest of the time I spend reading, writing, hiking, biking, dancing, thinking, traveling, dreaming, and conversing.

I'm not subsidized by my family or the government. Nor did I sell a company, ride the stock market, go viral, traffic human organs, or take an online course revealing the one secret that will make all your financial dreams come true.

Rather, I found a form of work that I genuinely enjoy. Work that does good, pays well, and doesn't monopolize my life.

"Found" isn't really the right word. I stumbled, tinkered, and charmed my way into this work. Year after year, I do it all again. Nothing is guaranteed, but this fact energizes me.

I don't have a permanent residence. At various points, all of my possessions have fit into a small storage unit, the back of a car, or a few plastic bins. When I tire of migrating, I settle down for a few months or longer. Then I pick up and move on, in pursuit of the people, nature, and activities I cherish most. No one place holds my heart. I am geographically polyamorous.

Relationships are my first safety net. Good health is my second. Savings are my third.

I may not earn much, but compared to how I spend, it's a ton.

I'm not conventionally rich. I'm dirtbag rich.

WHAT'S A DIRTBAG?

THE FIRST DIRTBAGS were hardcore rock climbers in Yosemite Valley who camped illegally, showered infrequently, and scavenged for meals. When they needed money, they'd leave the Valley to paint houses, wait tables, teach skiing, or even take a desk job: anything to refill their coffers and get back to the big walls. They lived like bums in pursuit of the good life.

Today dirtbags come in many flavors, not just "climber" and "white male." Some are trail runners, mountain bikers, long-distance hikers, backcountry skiers, cross-country cyclists, or endless-summer surfers. Others are dancers, slackliners, or perpetual travelers. All are passionate. All are extreme. None are what the mainstream would describe as "balanced."

Some dirtbags live in vans, trucks, or tents. Others couchsurf, hitchhike, or stay with friends. Some do pay rent: just not very much, and not for very long. For dirtbags, full-time, full-price rental contracts lie somewhere between a luxury and an obscenity.

Many dirtbags come from middle-class security. Some come from upper-class privilege. Others come from next to nothing.

All dirtbags revere nature, movement, and thrift. All struggle to fit into conventional society. All want to be left alone to do what they love, while they also yearn for membership in a tight-knit community of the similarly obsessed.

Many who lead such lives aren't aware of the label "dirtbag." Of those who are aware, many don't welcome its associations. I understand their aversion, but I like the term.

To me, being a dirtbag simply means that you're too busy following your bliss to worry about a little dirt under your nails. It means you're doing something right.

DIRTBAGGING IS UNSUSTAINABLE, AS IS NORMAL LIFE

UNFORTUNATELY, DIRTBAGGING IS unsustainable in the long run.
Traveling, adventuring, and living close to nature is undoubtedly fun and fulfilling—until you get seriously ill or injured, need to sleep or eat better, require comprehensive health insurance, want to save for retirement, get fed up with your menial seasonal jobs, fall in love with someone who's not a dirtbag, or start a family. Normal life and its promise of security begin to look awfully attractive when the wheels come off your vehicle or finding shelter becomes a real issue.

Unfortunately, for people like me (and perhaps you), normal life is also unsustainable in the long run.

If dirtbagging calls to you, then attempting to live normally is a brutal reminder of why you cannot accept the full-time job, the boss, the commute, the meetings, the bureaucracy, the accumulation of junk, the normalization of debt, and the never-ending postponing of life.

Your body rebels against all the sitting: at desks, in cars, on trains. Your mind rejects the barrage of advertisements and entertainments, the chorus of phones buzzing and vibrating, the endless splitting of attention. Even among friends and romantic partners, you feel isolated and alienated.

You might fit in, but you know you're out of place. You sense that something vital is being eroded, precious possibilities are being erased, and that you are growing old at an unacceptably early age.

Despite a growing bank account, you feel neither wealthy nor secure. You feel like a fraud.

THE CYCLE OF QUITTING BEGINS

I KNOW WHAT it's like to feel at loose ends. By age 24, I had failed at both dirtbagging and normal life.

Straight out of college, I landed a job at Astrocamp, an outdoor education center in the mountains of southern California. I got paid to take 5th-graders hiking, swing them on ropes through the forest, weave stories about the evolution of the universe, and conduct mad scientist experiments like freezing pennies with liquid nitrogen and smashing them to bits with a hammer.

As someone who loved nature, science, and working with kids, I was sure I'd found my dream job. But after just a few months, the repetitiveness wore me down. As soon as I got to know one student group, a bus whisked them away and another took their place. I was back to square one, saying the same things I had just said last week.

My gaze drifted toward the nearby Pacific Crest Trail, the famed walking path from Mexico to Canada. I had the gear and the guidebook, and with my discontent growing and spring around the corner, I had a reason to go. I gave a week's notice, hugged my co-workers goodbye, and hitched a ride to the Mexican border.

I'd never quit a job on such short notice. Part of me felt ashamed, but a larger part felt relieved. I had escaped the first hint of monotonous drudgery in my adult career. Now I was pursuing a higher calling:

hiking for five straight months through the deserts, forests, and mountains of California, Oregon, and Washington. Transcendent wilderness bliss, here I come!

Two weeks later, I quit the Pacific Crest Trail.

Despite the audiobooks I devoured and fellow hikers I befriended, it didn't take long for my romantic vision of immersion in pure nature to crumble. The hiking itself was manageable. What I couldn't handle was the monotony, disconnection from society, and unbearable stickiness of my sweaty, sunscreen-caked skin.

Final steps on the Pacific Crest Trail

Under Interstate 10 in Southern California, I hugged my hiker friends goodbye, hopped a train to the East Coast, and joined my brother working at a summer camp in Pennsylvania.

The cycle had begun.

A LOVE OF FLIGHT

SOON I BEGAN quitting almost everything that I started. After returning from the East Coast, I moved to South Lake Tahoe and committed to work a full year at a health food cafe. A month later, I left to teach snowboarding at a ski resort. A week later, I quit that job too, struck by the realization that I would spend an entire winter on the same handful of beginner runs.

I didn't even tell my boss when I left the snowboard school. I turned off my cell phone and drove the length of California, returning three days later after sleeping in my car at a gas station in Los Angeles and making a foolish, late-season attempt to hike Mount Whitney.

Back in South Lake Tahoe, my roommate Morgan hugged me and cried. "What happened?" she asked. "I don't know," I said, shaking my head. "I just had to go."

Growing up, I was always the good boy, the straight-A student, and the hard worker. Now I was in danger of becoming a full-blown flake. I wasn't even sticking to the things I thought I wanted most, like hiking the Pacific Crest Trail or becoming a snowboard instructor. Why was this happening? Was it because of my multi-household, multiple-divorce upbringing? Reading too much Kerouac? Some deep-seated fragility not even I was aware of?

I dreamed of pulling a Christopher McCandless and parking my car along a Forest Service road, walking into the woods, and living in a tent with a bag of rice and a stack of books until I made sense of life. But there was no rationalizing this impulse to flee. It would arrive seemingly from nowhere, like a tsunami. The calm seas of my life would recede, replaced by a towering wave of emotion, sweeping away whatever plans I had made.

I resolved to take another outdoor education job and definitely not quit. Which I did—until I returned for another season, only to find myself engulfed in another wave of panic. I left that job within 24 hours of the tsunami, placing a handwritten letter on my boss's doorstep, secured by a large rock to prevent the desert winds from bearing it away. It read:

> *Dear Brett,*
> *I quit. I'm sorry.*
> *—Blake*

Speeding north on Interstate 5, my heart raced with guilt, relief, and confusion. I was free again, but to what end? To make another commitment from which I would walk away? Whenever I spent too long in one place, the same feelings returned: *This is a trap. Flee, now!* To ignore these impulses felt like settling, and to settle was some unthinkable sin.

Flipping through the Lonely Planet guidebook *South America on a Shoestring* in a Seattle bookstore, I was reminded that as the northern days contracted, a southern summer dawned. I closed my eyes and imagined leaving the darkness behind in a streak of contrails.

Everything was happier in the summer. Everything worked in the summer. The only jobs I reliably held were summer camp jobs. When a college friend told me he was going to Buenos Aires, I took it as a sign. I had failed to realize my dirtbag dreams, and I was failing as a productive member of society. Whatever I needed to learn, I wasn't learning here. To escape this samsara, I had to make a break for it. I bought a one-way ticket to Ecuador with plans to meet my friend a few months later.

My mom cried as she dropped me off at the airport. "Will I ever see you again?" she asked.

"Of course," I told her.

All I really knew was that I had to go far, far away.

A DIFFERENT WAY

THE NEXT THREE months I hugged the spine of the Andes, moving steadily southward on the gringo trail. The ocean waves thrashed me in Máncora, the garbage trucks serenaded me in Arequipa, the salt flats mesmerized me in Uyuni, and the border crossing mystified me at La Quiaca. I fell for a Swiss woman in Perú, a Canadian woman in Bolivia, and the entire adult female population of Argentina. I searched for orcas on the Valdés Peninsula, discovered chocolate-coated nirvana in Bariloche, lost sleep in a 20-bed dorm in Buenos Aires, and found solace in a café cortado the morning after. Forehead pressed to the windows of long-distance buses, the fog in my brain evaporated, and I began to outline a new way forward: one that combined the dirtbag virtues of freedom, passion, and thrift with some of normal life's promised riches.

Flying back to California broke, tan, and happy, I lined up another string of outdoor education, summer camp, and ski resort jobs—the the same types of positions I'd previously fled. But I already knew I wouldn't return to my cycle of quitting, because South America had shown me what it was like to feel constantly in love rather than constantly trapped. That was going to become my new normal. It *had* to. I just needed to figure out how to get there.

I didn't want to become a parasite or grifter. Working to achieve basic financial independence was important to me. Yet I was clearly allergic to traditional, full-time employment. Even the famous 5-week paid vacations of Silicon Valley and Scandinavia now struck me as laughably short, yoked as they were to 40-hour (or longer) work weeks. If I wanted to take another long international journey, multi-week backpacking trip, or a spontaneous hike on a sunny weekday, I would not be denied. I was the owner of my life, and I would not let an employer dictate its terms.

I craved geographic flexibility. With family and friends scattered across North America, staying in any one place year-round meant sacrificing face time with many I loved. Despite my sudden break-up with the Pacific Crest Trail, I remained enamored with the mountains, forests, and deserts of the American West, desperately wanting to explore their every nook and cranny. And escaping the northern winter for a southern summer had shown me that my sun-spoiled California soul need not suffer when the days grew short. Remaining mobile and untethered would allow me to maintain my relationships, connection to wilderness, and climate-sensitive mental health.

Finally, my inner activist had reawakened. Three months of contemplation on Perú's overnight buses, inside Argentina's posh cafes, and amidst Bolivia's desolate beauty revealed a deep, obsessive need to fight for a social cause. In my case, this meant investigating and promoting alternatives to the creativity-crushing American school system, a mission I'd pursued passionately in college. My heart began telling me, gently but firmly, that a social purpose must take center stage.

In the year that followed my South American escape, my twenty-fifth on Earth, I began to map out a vision of a future I might not just tolerate but wholeheartedly embrace:

- If I rejected permanent residence in favor of a life on the road, I could stay close to friends, family, nature, sunshine, and the spirit of adventure.
- If I worked hard, spent little, and grew my savings without resorting to a full-time job, I might pass as a "productive member of society" while avoiding burnout.

- If I put a social cause at the center of my life, perhaps I'd finally have a strong enough reason to break the cycle of committing, quitting, and fleeing.

Many questions remained. How could I earn enough while only working part-time? How would I manage without a home base? What if I wanted a family? And beneath them all: What if I was making a giant, life-shattering mistake by not swallowing my discomfort, burying these impossible desires, and getting on with a normal existence?

I knew that every path has trade-offs. If I lived for adventure, I might not have kids. If I had kids, I'd certainly take fewer adventures. Travel would change me, just as rootedness would change me. Working for myself might be the best thing I ever do, and turning my passion into a business might suffocate it.

No one can have it all. But maybe, just maybe, I could have more than the world promised.

ABOUT THIS BOOK

IN THE 15+ years since I made that fateful decision, I've learned much about what it takes to become dirtbag rich. I've tweaked, refined, and pressure-tested my ideas in the mountains of New Zealand, on the highways of North America, and among the capital cities of Europe.

As I stumbled toward dirtbag riches in my twenties and thirties, I did not follow any particular formula or philosophy. Rather, I drew inspiration from the people I met, the books I read, and the solitudes of travel, wilderness, and journaling. Choosing this path meant encountering more than my fair share of charismatic figures who promised that my life would become amazing if I would only sell my possessions, start my own company, build passive income, become a digital nomad, or retire early. Each possessed some slice of the truth, but many lacked humility and intellectual honesty. I do not intend to contribute to this tradition. While this book is firmly rooted in my personal experience, it also contains stories and perspectives from others who have found their own balance of security, meaning, and adventure.

What do I mean by *dirtbag rich*? Currently I define it this way:

> a high-freedom, low-income lifestyle
> filled with nature, movement, and connection
> fueled by purposeful, well-paid, part-time work

Your version of dirtbag rich won't exactly match mine. We have different histories, personalities, aptitudes, and blind spots. What "purposeful" means to you differs for me, and that's okay. What matters are the fundamentals.

Whenever I pick up a book that offers life advice, I ask myself: *Do the author's struggles, hang-ups, and neuroses match my own?* If so, then maybe I have something useful to discover here.

In that spirit, here are some of the struggles, hang-ups, and neuroses I've navigated for most of my life:

- I feel more at home in transition than settled.
- What I call a love of freedom others seem to consider a disorder.
- I'm a lifelong skeptic of marriage—even as a child I said I'd prefer a civil union.
- Movement, travel, and exercise are how I cope with sadness, boredom, and grief.
- I've always needed to feel special, different, in charge of my life, and not a pawn in someone else's game.
- I cannot bear the thought of dying having spent most of my adulthood sitting indoors, working on something I don't believe in.

If this feels familiar, maybe you will discover something useful here.

And if it all feels a bit too serious and sober, let me emphasize: living dirtbag rich is a *hell* of a lot of fun.

You get to wake up when you want, and do what you want, most days of the year. You get to spend your youthful energy and express your physical vigor rather than bottling them up and watching them fade. You get to do work that matters, work that makes you feel good— and not too much of it. When others are stuck indoors on a sunny day, you get to grab your shoes, boots, skis, bike, or chalk and head into nature. You're not playing that same crazy game as everyone else, but you're not destitute, either. Online influencers feel a bit less influential, and self-care routines feel a bit less necessary, as the quality of your day-to-day existence improves. (No need for "life hacks" when the default software is running just fine.) You can dedicate more time to friends, lovers, community members, and family—and this energy is reflected back to you. On good days, you may even feel like you're navigating the contradictions inherent in modern capitalism.

Yes, it's possible. Yes, it's hard. Just like every other life choice, it's a question of what kind of glory you crave and what kind of difficulties you can face down.

This is my story. It's also an invitation.

Let's begin.

THIS IS WHAT I'M SUPPOSED TO DO?

SO THIS IS what I'm supposed to do: get married, buy a house, raise a kid, take a vacation?

Get a degree, get health insurance, get homeowner's insurance, get an accountant, get therapy?

Go to the gym, check my cholesterol, wait in line at the grocery store, watch entertaining shows, play entertaining games, stand around, make small talk, drink a beer?

Work for a stable company with benefits and bonuses? If I like the job—great? If the job contributes positively to the world—cool? But if neither is true—don't stress, because that's not the point? Because the point is to survive, reproduce, and be comfortable?

Maybe if I'm lucky, if I'm on top of my game, then I'll have enough time to read a book, learn a foreign language, dabble in spirituality, or tighten my abs?

Maybe if I'm lucky, I can stop working, get an RV, drive around, see the national parks, and then go home, tend the garden, watch some movies, and keep an eye on the investments?

Maybe if I'm lucky, the kids will visit, telling me tales of how they're on their way to some version of the same story?

This is it? This is what I'm supposed to do?

NOT MY KIND OF PARTY

LISTEN, THAT ALL sounds very nice. Thank you for the invitation. It's just not my kind of party.

I like to party. But parties take a lot of work. And this particular party—this version of human flourishing—requires a *lot* of supplies and a *lot* of clean-up.

I believe other people when they say, "I enjoy this existence."

I believe them when they say it's meaningful, they're built for it, and they can't imagine another way.

I even believe they're sincere when they say, "This is what our species is *supposed* to do."

Maybe I'm just not a very good member of our species.

Regular jobs, regular relationships, and regular ways of living haven't worked out for me. I'm not a great team player. I want to do my own thing. Always have.

Maybe I shouldn't reproduce. Maybe my genes should hit a dead end. If we humans are to better ourselves—if we are to survive on this thin crust of soil atop a barren rock hurtling through the void—maybe the non-team players should take a seat on the bench.

If that's true, then what's my point in existing? And if you're anything like me, what's your point of existing? What can people like us contribute to Team Human?

We can show each other a new way to party.

FIFTEEN HOURS A WEEK

A CENTURY AGO, a famed economist predicted that we'd be partying differently.

In 1930, John Maynard Keynes prophesied that 100 years later, the average citizen of a rich country (like his United Kingdom) would be eight times wealthier than one living today, working just 15 hours a week to cover the basics.

Keynes was right, and Keynes was wrong.

Most of us in rich countries today are much better off—materially speaking—than he assumed. Yet we still work 40+ hours a week.

How did this happen? How could we become vastly more wealthy than before and yet still find ourselves working just as much?

One big reason is that the "basics" now include modern healthcare (see: hospitals in 1930), modern housing (see: construction in 1930), modern transport (see: long journeys in 1930), and modern consumption (see: food and entertainment in 1930).

Once the basics expand, it's almost impossible to go back. In rich countries, you can't choose to live in a 1930s-quality dwelling or receive 1930s-quality healthcare. You probably can't even use a cell phone made a decade ago.

If you drastically reduced your standard of living while continuing to earn a modern wage, 15 hours a week would be more than enough. But that's called "living in squalor," and we've outlawed it.

As a society gets materially richer, it drags its members forward in the name of human dignity. This is called *progress*, and it's a rather good party. Many people die every day—crossing deserts on foot and oceans by raft—to join the progress party.

("Progress party" is my catch-all term for societies that become freer, richer, more secure, and more inclusive over time. It's not related to any actual political party.)

If you live somewhere that other people are willing to die to join, you should consider yourself lucky. But that doesn't mean you have to party the same way as everyone else.

Keynes recognized that material progress led to new possibilities for living:

> Thus for the first time since his creation man will be faced with his real, his permanent problem—how to use his freedom from pressing economic cares, how to occupy the leisure, which science and compound interest will have won for him, to live wisely and agreeably and well.
>
> The strenuous purposeful money-makers may carry all of us along with them into the lap of economic abundance. But it will be those peoples, who can keep alive, and cultivate into a fuller perfection, the art of life itself and do not sell themselves for the means of life, who will be able to enjoy the abundance when it comes.
>
> — "Economic Possibilities for our Grandchildren" (1930)

Here's what I believe: Keynes was more right than wrong.

You can live well today—shockingly well—on 15 hours a week of paid work. And this can be good, satisfying work. Work that doesn't immiserate yourself or others. Work that serves both yourself and your fellow human beings.

You can join the progress party just long enough to shake a few hands, kiss a few babies, snag some *hors d'oeuvres*, and then ghost—disappearing into the night to sleep under a blanket of stars.

THE POINT OF YOUR EXISTENCE

WHAT I'M SAYING is pretty simple: you can step just outside of society's guardrails. You can become the green sprout growing in the cracked edge of a concrete world.

Becoming dirtbag rich is not about tricking others into giving you something for nothing. We humans are natural traders and instinctively seek fair exchange. We resist entitlement and practice reciprocal altruism. No matter whether you call yourself a capitalist, socialist, anarchist, or something else, all political systems recognize the value of contributing to the larger whole.

We're groupish animals. Humans only made it this far by helping each other. "Work" is nothing more than people helping other people in a way that all parties recognize to be useful. This is why most any vision of opting out—of leaving normal society—must include some element of relationship, of being valued by others.

The point of our existence is to find the people, places, and modes of contributing that make us feel most alive—and to share that aliveness with others.

The enemy is not capitalism or communism or consumerism. It's zombie culture.

Zombies take from the living, offering nothing in return. Zombies think only of themselves. Zombies do not cooperate. Zombies have no vision of a better world.

Do not become a zombie. Stay alive.

I'm alive when I'm traveling, running, cycling—any time I'm moving my body through space. I'm alive when I write and dream. I'm alive when I wake in the mountains and witness a shaft of light breaking through the pine forest for a brief, fleeting moment.

I'm alive when I take teenagers on their first big international adventure. I'm alive when I run games at a summer camp, discuss books with friends, and teach skills that matter to people who care. I'm alive when I dance with others, write for others, dream with others, and share fleeting moments in nature with others.

This is the point of my existence. And I bet that it's the point of your existence, too—becoming as alive as possible.

YOU REALLY DON'T HAVE TO

AT AGE 20, I had an "a-ha" moment.
I was in college, studying physics and astronomy, thinking about becoming a high school science teacher, when I stumbled upon a few books by teachers who had quit the profession in frustration with the education system. Like intellectual cocaine, the words in these books electrified me. One of them, written by a New York City middle-school teacher who earned Teacher of the Year three times before quitting, captivated me so completely that I dropped everything and spent three days poring over it.

Within a few months, I decided to abandon the traditional teaching path and petitioned my university to let me create my own program of study: one that would let me study radical alternative schools, self-directed learning, and something called "unschooling." I convinced two professors to sponsor my plan, and the administration approved. I graduated with an obscurely titled bachelor's degree that commanded little value in the marketplace, but that didn't bother me. My mind was on fire.

The lesson I took from my deep dive into alternative education was this: *You don't have to.*

You don't have to go to school to become educated. You don't have to get a fancy degree (or possibly any degree) to find good work. You don't have to play by all the rules that feel so clear, compelling, and non-negotiable as a child. You can opt out of a very large, seemingly essential system, and your life will be fine—and possibly much, much better.

Prior to college, I had been a winner at the game of school. I graduated near the top of my class and was admitted to a well-regarded public university. But in truth I never quite fit the mold. Middle school and high school always felt like some sort of weird social experiment, holding chamber, or jail sentence, replete with tall fences, warring gangs, and campus police. What were we doing here? Why was the school day structured like this? Why did we have to learn this and not that? Why did students treat each other so badly, and when they did, why did most adults look the other way? There were no answers.

So when I started working with teenagers who opted out of the school system, we connected. In almost any other setting, most of these young people would have been labeled ADHD, socially anxious, neurodivergent, or oppositional-defiant. I found them hilarious, creative, authentic, and gloriously weird.

We connected because none of us felt like we belonged in that great homogenizer called school. We connected because we questioned the value of a major institution that most others embraced. And we connected because we knew that the monolithic commandment of childhood—*YOU MUST GO TO SCHOOL*—was actually a fiction.

If this was the case, then what other "musts" might be fictions?

Must we start college at age 18? Must we earn more than our parents or "keep up" with friends? Must we own homes? Must we spend our lives inside a climate-controlled room, sitting in a chair, staring at a glowing screen? Must gender dictate our social roles? Must we get married, have kids, date one person at a time, have lots of sex, be religious, not be religious, "use our education," maintain an online presence, or stay in one place?

As I entered my twenties and questioned ever-more "musts," I sensed my universe expanding. I hailed from a fundamentally conventional background. My Californian parents, each middle-class transplants from New England, were open-minded but not deeply norm-questioning. My dad read the *Wall Street Journal* and took pride in the successful food-processing business he had built. My mom had me at 22, my brother at 24, a divorce from my dad at 26, and returned to college to begin a career in human resources. My suburban upbringing was filled with computers, skateboards, video games, shopping malls, and *Magic: the Gathering* cards. No one in my young life nudged me down a radical path. Left to my default settings, I probably would have become a tech geek living in the San Francisco Bay Area who hiked on the weekends.

Instead, here I am on this strange and wonderful path: working as much as Keynes prophesied for almost two decades, with friends around the world, adventures under my belt, money in the bank, and a spirit that remains fully alive.

I'm here to tell you, as a few ex-teachers once told me, that you don't have to play the same game as everyone else. You can throw your own party. You can have a life where you wake up and decide what you want to do, every day.

You really can.

THE CURRENCY OF FREEDOM

THE MAGIC TRIFECTA

IMAGINE THREE RESOURCES: time, money, and purpose.

Different parts of life demand a different balance of these resources.

When you're a new parent, you sacrifice time and money—and sleep, and happiness, and sex—for the deeper purpose of raising children.

When you're new to the workplace, you accept low pay and questionable purpose for the time needed to build your skills, wisdom, and connections.

The vast majority of normal, working adults focus on making money at the expense of time and purpose, which they hope to reclaim in retirement.

The dirtbag rich are non-normal individuals who cling to a wholly unreasonable vision of life: they want time, money, and purpose—and they want it all *now*.

Some hold the title of writer, guide, sailor, artist, nurse, teacher, speaker, consultant, photographer, programmer, event organizer, or public school employee. All of them desire meaningful work that leaves plenty of time for their favorite activities, while also earning enough to pay their bills and save something for the future.

Specifically, the dirtbag rich prioritize:

Time Flexibility: Remaining in control of the hours of their day, week, or year—which might look like working regularly but part-time, working intensely but seasonally, or having an otherwise normal job that allows significant breaks. Some people need more flexibility, some need less. However it happens, the point is to maintain one's mental health and avoid even the slightest whiff of eternal servitude.

Good Pay + Low Expenses: By earning a substantial amount relative to their efforts—via a high hourly wage, big payouts after big gigs, or some version of so-called passive income—the dirtbag rich can afford not to work full-time. But this only works because they keep their expenses low. Many dirtbag rich could earn a six-figure salary if they worked full-time. Instead, they deliberately subsist on a lower income, sometimes even "poverty wages," to enjoy the time required to do what they love. It feels paradoxical, but the dirtbag rich are both "high pay" and "low income" at the same time.

Deep Purpose: Finally, the dirtbag rich organize their lives to find meaning in both their paid work and free-time activities. They don't make purpose wait for the weekend or retirement. They do what moves them, compensated or not, day in and day out. This is the ultimate reason for carefully managing their time and money.

The dirtbag rich aren't entrepreneurial geniuses or superhuman freaks. They're financially savvy do-gooders who want to spend their healthiest years moving their bodies, living close to nature, and making meaningful contributions to the world today, not tomorrow, and certainly not in some mythical, old-age utopia. They want time, money, and purpose, just like everyone else does. But they're the ones who are weird, lucky, and determined enough—sometimes even sleeping in the dirt, in a bag—to make this vision real.

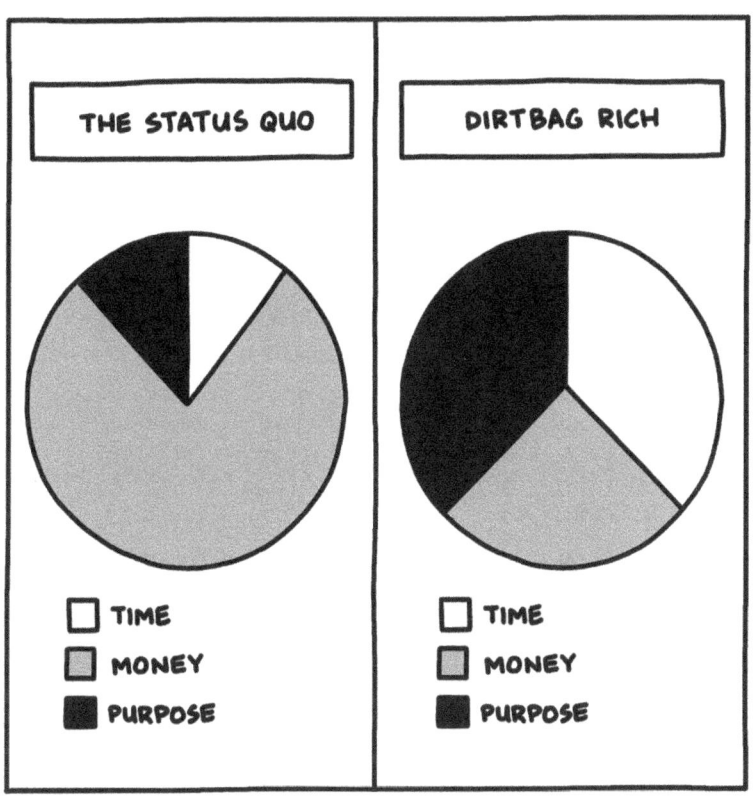

BUILD YOUR OWN ESCAPE HATCH

"**SOUNDS GREAT,**" you may think while perched nervously at your first desk job, contemplating years of servitude, or having recently fled a dead-end situation. "But how does it begin? How does one go from dreaming of dirtbag riches to taking the first steps?"

Shortly after my trip to South America—the one that helped me escape the vicious cycle of quitting and fleeing—I returned to South Lake Tahoe, California, and rented a cheap spare room from an older divorcée. A former roommate helped me get a job in marketing research at the ski resort, which let me snowboard around the mountain all day, cut lift lines, and interview people on chairlifts. When the lifts closed, I would retreat to my little room, crack open my laptop, and continue working on the manuscript I started in South America: a guidebook for teenagers who hated school but still wanted to go to college. I mashed the keyboard until my brain stopped functioning and then made dinner, strummed my guitar, buried my nose in a book, or swam in the local pool. It was a beautiful, low-income, dirtbaggy existence—and an existence that I absolutely had to leave behind.

The ski resort job was fun, but I didn't see a future there. Full-time writing didn't seem like a viable career path. I had lots of experience working at summer camps and outdoor education centers, but becoming an administrator in such a program seemed like just another way to trap myself in an office and miss out on the parts I loved most: being outside, using my body, and working directly with young people. I wanted more money, more responsibility, more fun, and minimal compromise.

An online search led me to a three-month international trip leader position for a gap year company: the closest thing I could imagine to a dream job. They wanted someone who was 25, spoke Spanish, and held outdoor medical certifications—check, bueno, check. The pay wasn't great ($4,000 for twelve weeks), but the job covered all my expenses, so at least I'd save everything I earned. I filled out the application, flew through the interviews, and felt confident about getting the position. A few weeks later, the director emailed me to say that 200 people had applied for five positions, and while I was clearly qualified, I wasn't selected.

That hurt. I really wanted that job. I'd already envisioned leading young people across some sunny foreign country, getting paid to expand minds while I expanded my own world at the same time. I stewed in my little room in South Lake Tahoe for a few weeks, and then I stopped and asked myself: "What if I just did it anyway?"

I called my friend Abbi, who also worked at the summer camp for self-directed teenagers where I'd served for a few years, and I asked her: "Want to take a group of teens to Argentina together?" She was in. Then I emailed the director of the gap year company—the same one who rejected me, but with whom I clicked during the interviews—and told him I was thinking about starting a travel program for unschooled teenagers. "Would you help me answer a few tricky questions about group flights, health insurance, student medications, and liability concerns?" It was a wild gamble, and to my unending surprise and delight, he said yes, he'd love to help—because he believes the world needs more youth travel opportunities.

Within a month I'd registered a new company, opened a business bank account, and created a basic website. Abbi and I spread the word about our 6-week "Unschool Adventure" within our summer camp community and Abbi's unschooling contacts. We ended up recruiting nine teenagers, had a blast from Patagonia to Buenos Aires, brought everyone home safely, and stayed within budget. Abbi and I each took home $4,000: the same amount that I would have earned working twice as long for the gap year company—minus the creative control.

I stretched that $4,000 across four months of urban living in Portland, Oregon: staying in a cheap rented room, reading endlessly at Powell's Bookstore, taking Argentine tango classes (a new love I'd discovered in Buenos Aires), and toying with another business idea which I'd soon abandon. When my bank account reached critical levels, I retreated to familiar territory, taking an outdoor education gig on the East Coast for a few months. Two steps forward, one step back.

I was 26, living on $10-$15,000/year, and not saving much. But my fortunes were rising in other ways. A small Canadian publisher had purchased my book manuscript, providing me with a bit of money and sufficient credibility to begin a side career as a public speaker at homeschooling conferences and alternative schools (which doubled as a recruiting tool for Unschool Adventures). I was beginning to pay my bills with progressively fewer hours of work, and the work itself was feeling increasingly purposeful.

I'd found the escape hatch from my previous, unsustainable existence. I hadn't yet reached the cruising altitude of dirtbag rich, but at least I was moving vertically through the troposphere of time, money, and purpose.

BE MORE SPECIAL

ACH PERSON'S LAUNCH sequence is unique. Please don't follow in my footsteps. (I disavow responsibility for any teenagers misplaced abroad.) But there *is* a general trajectory toward dirtbag riches, and it's one you can follow.

I know this because, after years of encountering other dirtbag rich types and asking, "How the heck did you get here," I began formally interviewing them. What resulted was a public repository of one-on-one conversations with working adults who had achieved a magical balance of time, money, and purpose, with an emphasis on spending lots of time in nature. I spoke with nomads and homeowners, single moms and stay-at-home dads, outdoor guides and freelance photographers, serial entrepreneurs and travel nurses, foster-care families and childfree couples—none of whom were trust fund babies or enabled by wealthy partners. Each exhibited a different flavor of this lifestyle, and each helped me escape the bubble of my own experience.

What I learned from these conversations was this: Whether employed or self-employed, every member of the dirtbag rich had done a very good job of making themselves *extremely special* in one little corner of the global economy. They had achieved a combination of pay, purpose, and flexibility by taking—and more often, creating—an economic role that few or no others can fill.

Here's the approximate trajectory I observed:

1. Discover a form of discomfort that you uniquely enjoy
2. Seize opportunities to rapidly build skills without spending much money
3. Connect your skills to an underserved audience that also has the ability to pay
4. Tweak, refine, and improve your offering—and keep charging a bit more—until you find the right balance of time and money

In my case, working at summer camp was a form of discomfort that I uniquely enjoyed. Living in a tent for months on end, taking 12-year-olds on their first backpacking trips, facilitating groups of moody teenagers: bring it on! Most other twenty-somethings had no desire to live such a life, or if they did, one summer was enough. Each season that I returned to work at the two summer camps in my life—an off-grid children's wilderness camp in California and the camp for teenage unschoolers—I took on more responsibilities, built new skills, and saved most of what I earned. My South American escapade had also shown me that the challenges of extended foreign travel—like navigating language barriers, noisy hostels, and 24-hour bus rides—were my kind of suffering. Traveling cheaply, staying organized, and managing risk came naturally to me. Between this and the camp work, I was well-positioned to run my first group trip to Argentina.

But I also knew that talent and enthusiasm weren't enough to get a small business off the ground. To do something really special—and earn accordingly—meant connecting with an underserved audience that would happily pay for the unique opportunities I might offer.

At the camp for unschoolers, there were many teenagers who thirsted for bigger adventures. And while countless travel programs existed for high schoolers, virtually no such opportunities existed for those who didn't go to school (and could therefore travel during the school year). I sensed an opportunity and performed some back-of-the-envelope calculations. The unschooling camp cost about $1000, plus travel, for two weeks. My Argentina trip would cost participants $3500, plus travel, for six weeks. I was in the right ballpark, and compared to established teen travel programs, my trip was a downright bargain. Unlike a summer camp, I didn't need 50 or 100 sign-ups to turn a profit—I just needed eight. And most importantly, I could run my little experiment with minimal start-up costs. If we didn't get enough participants to run a profitable trip, we simply wouldn't run the trip.

After the first trip to Argentina, I planned another adventure in Australia. I budgeted better, charged a bit more, took 11 teens instead of nine, and ended up earning twice as much money.

A few years later, I found the sweet spot: running 6-week trips with 12 participants and 2-3 trip leaders, at the cost of $4000-5000 per participant. If all went well, I could run two such programs a year—approximately three months of full-time work, plus around 40 total planning hours—and take home $30-40k. Throw in a little income from writing, speaking, and brief camp gigs (all of which helped attract teen trip applicants), and by my early thirties I was earning $40-50k/year—more than enough to cover my costs, save generously, and still spend most of my year writing, traveling, dancing, and taking wilderness adventures.

Cruising altitude: achieved.

That's my story. If it speaks to you, wonderful. If it doesn't, you'll find other examples in the upcoming chapters. After listening to a handful of stories, you'll notice that the dirtbag rich are those who:

- Run toward suffering and discomfort, not away from it, as long as it's on their own terms (much like a long-distance hiker or low-budget traveler)
- Deepen their skills through paid work and personal experiments rather than expensive training or degrees (which may be socially validated but ultimately unnecessary)
- Connect with a niche audience whose problems they understand and then give special attention to the segment that can pay a bit more (as I did with teenage unschoolers)
- Continue charging more money over time until the market, their conscience, and their calendar say "that's enough"

Even the dirtbag rich who are traditionally employed tend to look at their jobs through the lens of entrepreneurship. In other words, they see themselves as—and take the steps necessary to become—equal negotiating partners with their employers.

If entrepreneurship is new territory for you, I suggest reading a few good books about small business, start-ups, and freelancing. I'm certainly glad I read such books in my mid-twenties. But be warned: such books typically assume that you want to work full-time and don't place an especially high premium on purpose. Traditional self-employment can induce burnout as quickly as traditional employment.

Your economic engine is only as powerful as the freedom it generates. No matter whether you're employed or self-employed, focus on offering something you care deeply about, to people who care about you, while making good money and not monopolizing your life. This is how to become truly special.

LIFESTYLES OF THE DIRTBAG RICH AND FAMOUS

AS SOON AS anyone starts talking about making more money in less time, it's important to get into the nitty-gritty. Are the dirtbag rich just shrewd entrepreneurs who sell stuff to rich people? Is focusing on "the ability to pay" a dog whistle for ignoring the poor and working class? Whose purpose are we really considering here?

When I started running programs for teenagers whose families could pay $5000 for life-enriching travel opportunities, I remained carefully attuned to the possibility that I'd end up serving entitled kids.

This possibility did not attract me. Having worked with both public and private schools as an outdoor educator, I knew the signs and symptoms of entitlement. I didn't want to work with teenagers who took travel for granted, treated less-resourced people with disdain, or refused to put themselves into uncomfortable situations that led to genuine growth, empathy, and shifted perspective.

In other words, if I was just going to help rich kids do more rich kid stuff, I wouldn't keep doing this for very long.

By carefully interviewing every applicant, never making things too easy for the teens, and only offering trips with weird, growth-oriented missions (rather than mere vacations), I've managed to avoid this fate. Yes, I still work with families who can afford this kind of thing. But most of the teens who show up on Unschool Adventures trips don't receive these kinds of opportunities very often. Many work to pay for part (or all) of their trip. Some have never left the country before. And nearly all are humble, kind, and open-minded—the very opposite of entitled.

Consider a thought experiment. Let's say you're extremely talented at retrofitting luxury vehicles. You enjoy the work, it makes your customers happy, you earn good money, and then you get to spend lots of time paragliding (or whatever). Is this "okay?"

From a certain perspective, it's fine. You're not actively harming, tricking, or defrauding anyone. You're undoubtedly improving the lives of a few luxury vehicle owners.

But for me and the dirtbag rich I admire most, working toward a clear social cause is preferable—because we sleep better, work harder, and feel better about ourselves when we're making a positive dent in the world.

Finding meaningful work isn't always easy, and most of us will traverse a wide spectrum of purposefulness over our careers. Some of my interview subjects are genuinely content with their ambiguously purposeful (but well-compensated and highly flexible) modes of employment. But most of us only feel truly rich when we've found the sweet spot: doing work that genuinely helps people, pays well, and doesn't demand all of our time.

Here are some of the stories of those who have achieved this precarious balance. Every name in **bold** is a *Dirtbag Rich* interview subject whose full story you can find online at blakeboles.com.

I met **Hannah Bowley** while biking through Seattle. A speech language therapist with Seattle Public Schools, Hannah was combing through her employment contract one day when she realized that she could take a year of unpaid leave after every three years of work. When she and I met, Hannah was preparing for a full year's cycling adventure across Europe, Asia, and South America: an adventure that I got to join when we teamed up to ride the Carretera Austral in Patagonia! Hannah adored her unpaid year of adventure, and when she returned to her speech language position, she was also very happy—because she considers her work both personally meaningful and socially important. She's already planning her next year away.

Then there's **Tim and Angel Mathis**, a married couple who each work part-time as nurses. Tim and Angel intentionally take the minimum number of shifts and contracts necessary to fuel their lives as long-distance hikers, runners, paddlers, and expat travelers. They also dedicate significant time toward their side-gigs as writers and educators. Tim is the author of multiple books, including *The Dirtbag's Guide to Life* (in which he coined the phrase "dirtbag rich"), and Angel teaches money management to other nurses. Like Hannah, Tim and Angel feel like they're making an important contribution to society through their nursing while simultaneously refusing to participate in standard, work-till-you-drop employment.

My friend **Jack Schott** adores summer camp and believes that it's a powerful force for good in the world. After a two-year road trip in his mid-twenties to visit hundreds of camps, followed by multiple summers of co-directing his own camp, Jack began working as a part-time communications facilitator for manufacturing business executives. "I pretty much put on a business costume, play camp games with them, and help them share their feelings," Jack told me. "I get paid $1500-$3500 a day for the chance to show executives how to be more human." Leading just a few such trainings each month, for a few months each year, provides Jack with enough money to fuel his travels, save up for creating his next camp, and create the mental and emotional space necessary to continue dreaming and scheming about transforming young lives through communal living in the outdoors.

Hannah, Tim, Angel, Jack, and I are the kind of people who need to get our hands dirty in the "helping fields" and feel the fruits of our labor directly. Other members of the dirtbag rich find purpose in a more roundabout way by employing their technical skills to serve a cause in which they believe.

Russell Max Simon is a rock climber whose content marketing skills (developed while working for political nonprofits in Washington, DC) support a nationwide network of doctors. Russell could easily earn more by taking his skills to larger organizations, but he sleeps better knowing that his work contributes to improving access to healthcare. Russell works about 15 hours a week and spends the rest of his time climbing, fixing up two old properties he bought adjacent to popular climbing areas, and playing host to the itinerant dirtbags who regularly appear on his doorstep.

Brittany Goris is one of those dirtbags—but one who has figured out how to lead life more sustainably than the average van-dwelling climber. Brittany works remotely as a graphic designer for an organization that helps young women enter STEM (science, technology, engineering, and mathematics) fields, averaging 15 hours a week from wherever she can scrounge up mobile data. Combined with a little extra income from gear sponsorships and teaching climbing clinics, Brittany has filled her life with more than a decade of outdoor adventure in North America and beyond.

The dirtbag rich come in many shapes and sizes. Some work for traditional companies; many work for themselves. Some own property; others own only what fits in their vehicle. But you'll never meet a dirtbag rich arms dealer, tobacco sales representative, or predatory lender. Because one thing that connects all of them, apart from the desire to play more than they work, is the desire to do something clearly good (or at least, clearly not harmful) for society.

Earn progressively more, work progressively less, stay flexible, and continue contributing to the human project, whether directly or indirectly—do this, and you're on the right path.

THE LIFE-CHANGING MAGIC OF BEING A NATURE-LOVING TIGHTWAD

IT DOESN'T MATTER how much money you make if you just go and spend it all. That's why another feature of the dirtbag rich is a diehard sense of thrift.

The number one act of frugality I've noticed among my interview subjects is this: seldom eating out or going to bars.

Number two: not accumulating much stuff.

Number three: not paying high rent.

I'm not here to say you can't drink nice coffee, own fancy running shoes, or enjoy a decent apartment. (I indulge in all three from time to time.) But instead of exploring the well-worn territory of "living cheaply," let's focus on a more upstream question: *How are you spending the time of your life?*

A dirtbag is someone who derives powerful meaning and satisfaction from the simple act of spending time outdoors, whether solo or socially. She can happily occupy herself with long hours of hiking, running, swimming, cycling, slacklining, backpacking, frisbee, surfing, climbing, or acroyoga. But what separates a dirtbag from a regular nature-lover is *how long she can enjoy herself* with limited resources.

Consider outdoor gear. It's easy to obsess over finding the right tent, the best paddleboard, or the perfect campervan. But most outdoor enthusiasts will only use their gear a few times and then park it in the driveway, closet, or garage—because while they may have plenty of money, they lack the time for long-term adventure.

Dirtbags, on the other hand, are obsessed with the question, "How far can I stretch this gear?" They are interested in how much joy they can derive from a single set of hiking poles, running shoes, or bicycle tires. How many adventures can one backpack, water filter, or rain jacket bring them? That's why compulsive gear accumulation is not the way of the dirtbag rich. What we ultimately care about is working less, needing less money, and having more time to do what we love—not purchasing items that symbolize the activities we wish we could do.

What about artists, musicians, or writers? There are many ways to pursue a high-freedom, low-income, and high-purpose life. Must you be a nature-lover to take the dirtbag rich path?

If you're someone who happily dwells in big cities or has no deep need for wilderness, you'll still find that much of the advice in this book applies to you. But it's also true that moving your body through the wild places of the world, often to the point of exhaustion, is the quintessential low-cost, high-purpose activity that connects the dirtbag rich. River-lovers, mountain-lovers, desert-lovers, and ocean-lovers intuitively grasp each other's obsessions—because each possesses a visceral, profound, and quasi-spiritual connection to the natural world.

Not everyone can easily or safely access the wilderness, and many people simply don't like (or haven't yet found a way to navigate) the bugs, sweat, dirt, weather, and discomfort inherent to spending extended time in nature. You don't necessarily have to love camping or hiking to be dirtbag rich, but the more you can get your kicks in the out-of-doors—and thereby avoid the costs of entertaining yourself in a big city—the less you must spend, and the more flexible you become.

No matter whether you're based in a big city, small town, or rural area, the dirtbag ethic of "simple pleasures" touches all modes of entertainment. Ask yourself: can you spend a satisfying evening cooking a meal, reading a book, making music, catching up with a friend, watching an old movie, writing, drawing, dancing, walking, painting, or meditating? Do you need to go out, buy a meal, or see a show to feel engaged? Are "meaningful memories" and "spending money" linked in your brain? That's a link the dirtbag rich have severed long ago.

I once ran a program in Berlin for 20 North American teenagers focused on discovering and creating "low-cost good times" in an otherwise expensive capital city. The teens discovered free concerts, went thrifting, climbed trees, played games and hosted picnics in parks, created art with cheap materials, took public transport to the end of the line, and even filmed their own horror movie in the hostel. Adventure is everywhere, they learned, if you only have the eyes to see it.

Frugality isn't just about discipline and creativity—it's also about social pressure. Do you have friends or family who badger you into joining them at fancy restaurants, hip bars, or costly vacations? Can you say "no" to them without breaking the connection? Can you redirect their energy toward more affordable alternatives without being shamed?

Let's say it again: those of us who pursue dirtbag riches are *not* normal people. We are obsessive, obstinate, individualistic, allergic to many social norms, and wary of conventional status symbols. We're the ones finishing the food on a friend's plate or wearing the same outfit multiple days in a row, oblivious to (or not minding) the glances coming from other people.

Many people live this way in their early twenties and then "grow out of it." The dirtbag rich are those who *never* stop living like frugal twenty-somethings, even as their incomes rise. They discover certain simple pleasures early in life, double down on them, and refuse to run on the same hedonic treadmill as everyone else.

Sure, their tastes evolve over time. The dirtbag rich dream of bigger and more ambitious adventures that require more money. But fundamentally, they need little more than good health, spacious free time, and like-minded companions to feel like they're making the most of life.

My own everyday pleasures include:

- Taking a walk with a podcast or audiobook
- Going for a long hike, trail run, or short backpacking trip
- Throwing a frisbee or slacklining in a public park
- Writing in a cafe, university library, or outdoor spot
- Social partner dancing
- Following a home-based yoga or workout video
- Riding a bicycle across a city (or between cities)
- Enjoying a long conversation with a friend over coffee, beer, tea, wine, or a simple dinner I've prepared

In the end, the arithmetic is simple: every dollar you refuse to spend is one less dollar you must earn—and one more dollop of bliss on the ice cream sundae which is your life.

PAY LESS FOR HOUSING

WHAT ABOUT HOUSING? To become dirtbag rich, must you sleep in a van, crash on a friend's couch, or live in a shoebox? Can you still be a normal person with a normal house or apartment?

While you don't have to sleep in the dirt, it's unreasonable to think that you can live this way while also enjoying a normal house or apartment in a rich country—because "normal" typically means spending a third (or more) of a standard, full-time income on rent, and you probably don't make that much money.

Depending on your personality, aptitudes, and circumstances, there are many ways to approach housing as an aspiring member of the dirtbag rich.

Paying little, owning little, and moving frequently

This is my own approach, and one that matches the dreaded dirtbag stereotype: bouncing between friends, renting temporary accommodations, camping and housesitting, taking advantage of employer-provided housing, and staying with friendly strangers through hospitality networks like Couchsurfing.

Some call this "bumming around." I prefer to think of it as "full-spectrum accommodation for those with itchy feet." It's a great choice for anyone who is easy-going, adaptable, social, self-sufficient, and already possesses a wide network of friends and family. As long as you can handle the logistics, living this way makes every day feel like an adventure.

As your income rises, it's nice to purchase a bit more privacy in the form of short-term rentals. My favorite rentals have included a rustic cabin in South Lake Tahoe, a clean room in an communal house of outdoorsy service workers in New Zealand, and some beautifully furnished (and surprisingly affordable) apartments in Europe and Argentina.

When you own next to nothing, moving in and out is simple, and not worrying about utilities or repairs is delightful. You can enjoy your little island of privacy and stability, and then hit the road again with your batteries charged.

But you will *always* be hitting the road again, sooner or later. Which is why this approach to housing is best suited for those who genuinely enjoy sleeping in strange places, transitioning frequently, searching for deals, making new friends, and forever finding ways to be helpful to your hosts—like cooking a meal, caring for children, tidying a kitchen, or fixing something that's broken—without being asked.

At its best, living this way is a fun, challenging, and never-ending jigsaw puzzle that, if played well, earns you a comfy night's sleep, deepened social connections, rich memories, and money in the bank. And if you circle back to the same places over time, you can become a genuinely valued member of multiple communities around the world—my favorite aspect of living this way.

But this approach can also be done poorly. If you witness yourself (or are told that you are) overstaying your welcome, abusing others' goodwill, or acting from a place of desperation rather than connection, then it's time to take a different path.

Home on wheels

Vanlife, truck life, RV life, and other forms of long-term car camping are time-honored dirtbag approaches, especially when paired with a period of diehard climbing, skiing, trail running, or long-term travel. It's also something that most people do for a limited time and then leave behind, out of a very reasonable desire for more consistent water, electricity, internet, cooking facilities, and personal space.

The social experience of living out of a vehicle can be both extraordinarily rewarding (when you're immersed in a community of like-minded travelers) and horribly isolating (when you're suddenly evicted by police, judged by passerbys, or creeped on by trollers). Long-term vehicle-dwellers don't typically spend all their time on the road, but instead migrate from one familiar driveway to the next, splitting their travels and rootedness fifty-fifty.

Once you're dialed into a network of friendly hosts—often centered on a particular outdoor activity, like skiing, climbing, or backpacking—living this way can be sweet. You're on the road for a while, you're crashing with friends for a while, you're going on adventures with these friends, and then you're on your own again.

And when life on the road eventually wears thin, as it did for vanlifer **Kaya Lindsay** after four years of constant migration between climbing meccas like Bishop, Squamish, and Indian Creek, you can complete the circle. Settle down in your favorite outdoor hub (like Kaya's beloved Moab), rent a modest house, fill it with roommates, and play host to the next generation of dirtbag vanlife climbers. Kaya also co-founded Moab's first climbing gym, ensuring that she always knows enough nice people who might become roommates and help pay the monthly bills.

Living abroad

Whether you go full-expat or just relocate to a foreign country for a few months, living abroad is a time-honored strategy of vagabonds, artists, writers, adventurers, and cash-strapped families with digital livelihoods.

Kelsey Shipman and her husband are educators who spent a lot of time working abroad before returning to their native state of Texas.

Despite earning a combined six figures in Austin, they were nonetheless stressed by their daily commute and the skyrocketing cost of childcare. So they relocated to San Miguel de Allende, Mexico, where they could finally afford high-quality childcare, a rental house within walking distance to their kid's school, and most importantly, the chance to reduce their working hours. Now Kelsey can write her book, her husband can spend more time with their child at home, and their family in Texas remains a short flight away.

Or there's **Peter Kowalke**, a US-born relationship coach who traveled extensively as a digital nomad, considers himself intentionally homeless, and spends a lot of time in Bangkok. Thailand's lower cost of living allows him to worry less about money, focus more on his coaching and spiritual practice—he calls himself a "half-monk"—and host regular dinner parties that bring together both his local friends and the international travelers he regularly meets.

Climbing the property ladder

Finally, some of the dirtbag rich do make the leap into homeownership, usually by purchasing lower-priced properties in desirable locations, fixing them up, and renting them out while continuing to live simply and frugally.

Among such types, my friend **Jenny Abegg**'s story is typical:

> I've always been against paying for rent. For a long time I lived in closets, cordoned-off parts of basements, and a van called "Ol' Blue." My costs were super low, so I was always able to save, even when I didn't earn much. When I bought my first house in Bend, Oregon, I immediately moved into the garage and kept the tenants in the main 4-bedroom house. I got lucky buying it when I did, because it doubled in value without needing any major repairs. So I did it again—I left Bend, took out some equity, and bought another little

house in Leavenworth, Washington. I converted the back bedroom into its own unit and quickly found a tenant. Now I have two houses, and my renters pay for both mortgages.

Jenny didn't make some grand, decade-long, burnout-inducing sacrifice to become a homeowner. She gathered her first down payment while working 20 hours remotely each week for an outdoor publication, while also enjoying more climbing, trail running, and peak-bagging than anyone I know. For Jenny, sleeping in a closet while saving for a down payment was a fun game to play, and a game that didn't restrict her ability to enjoy life now.

Another dirtbag rich "property baron" (my term) is **Artec Durham**, who finished nursing school debt-free at age 29 after years of working as an outdoor guide and trail crew member. By that point, Artec was so comfortable with dumpster-diving, living out of a vehicle, and finding ultra-cheap room rentals that it took him only one year of full-time nursing (saving 50% of his income) to afford his first down payment on a house in Flagstaff, Arizona. Like Jenny, he immediately fixed it up, filled it with housemates, and bought another property. Soon he could support himself with just 2-3 nursing shifts a month and spend the majority of his time doing what he loves most: mountain biking and bikepack racing.

My hat is off to Jenny, Artec, and anyone else who manages to build equity without sacrificing adventure (and doesn't rely on the Bank of Mom and Dad to pull it off). Jenny and Artec are also the first to admit that things could have gone much differently for them if they didn't get lucky with the housing market, or if one of their properties unexpectedly transformed into a bottomless money pit.

Unlike regular homeowners, dirtbag rich property owners don't look at their houses as oversized storage units to fill with new toys, furniture, and clothing. They carefully avoid "lifestyle creep" by viewing their properties as practical investments that enable their time-rich, outdoor-focused lives, rather than letting property management *become* their lives. They're also enthusiastic about sharing space, creating community, and living alongside roommates, rather than assuming that every square foot is their little fiefdom.

No matter whether you're living modestly with housemates, enjoying a home on wheels, temporarily ensconced in a foreign land, or choosing to play the homeownership game, remember this: there is plenty of time in life for nesting. Saving some resources for the future is important, but it's also important to take full advantage of the period in life when you'll happily sleep in strange places, seize wild opportunities, and trade discomfort for adventure. Energy, adaptability, and optimism are priceless resources. Do not trade them away for a couch, rug, and television.

GET CREATIVE WITH HUMAN SERVICES

BEYOND HOUSING, there are a few more costs that have the potential to derail a dream of dirtbag riches: healthcare, childcare, college tuition, and eldercare.

What's the connection? Each is a hands-on, human service that hasn't yet been wildly transformed by technology.

While the world has become richer in so many ways over the past centuries, this is most true regarding physical goods like electronics, clothing, cars, furnishings, and food. Today, you simply don't have to work as long or hard to earn such things as you would have 50 or 100 years ago. And the goods today are vastly superior.

Thanks to an obscure economic principle called "Baumol's cost disease," the decreasing cost of mass-produced goods leads to rising costs in sectors that haven't yet been revolutionized by machines or software, such as schooling, childcare, or home health assistance. That's why human services will only keep getting pricier (at least until the robots take over).

Paying full fare for healthcare, childcare, college tuition, or eldercare will derail your dreams as quickly as paying high rent. To combat this fate, you'll need some combination of luck and creativity. The main ways I've witnessed the dirtbag rich accomplish this include:

- Discovering (or creating) low-cost alternatives
- Relocating to places they can afford
- Relying on government subsidies
- Being fortunate enough not to need these services

Healthcare

Over the years I've had barebones healthcare policies, robust full policies, and sometimes, no policy. Fortunately, being a citizen of a rich country almost always means that if you don't earn much, you also don't pay much for healthcare. That's an amazing fact, and one that I gratefully exploit. In return, I play my part by virtually never accessing the healthcare system, thanks to a combination of lucky genes and actively prioritizing my health.

Disaster can always strike, of course, and no one should rely upon luck alone. When otherwise healthy **Courtney Bierschbach** discovered a cancerous lump on her throat in her thirties, both she and her husband were flexibly self-employed, which was both a blessing and a curse:

> [Self-employment] means no sick pay, no paid time off, and no Family and Medical Leave Act. Not just the initial surgeries, but driving to and from doctor's appointments, combined with generally feeling terrible, meant that I really couldn't do my job in the same way. It was a pretty big curveball and drained our rainy day fund. But I had built such solid relationships with my clients that every single one of them said, "Work when you can. We understand that you'll have good days and bad days. That's fine."
>
> As a business owner, I've always known I have lots of autonomy. But to hear this from my clients in such a graceful and respectful way really solidified that I had built strong relationships, and that it was going to be

okay. My clients weren't going to just disappear into the abyss. I could take the time that I needed to heal and recover. Now I'm cancer-free, going on two years.

Many people fearfully and incorrectly believe that without a "real job," they'll have no health coverage. Not true. Depending on your body, income, and risk tolerance, healthcare is likely to be just another line in your budget, and not necessarily the biggest one.

Courtney recommends a three-part approach: pay for health insurance, build a rainy day fund, and count on relationships. "The health insurance prevented me from having to pay $30,000 for each of my multiple surgeries, the savings covered my everyday costs while I took a break from working, and the relationships gave me something to 'get back to' and the peace of mind I needed to focus on healing."

Childcare

Yes, the dirtbag rich can and do start families. It's not simple or straightforward—this is a subject we'll revisit later in the book—but one thing is clear: building a life that's rich in time is incredibly handy for avoiding overpriced childcare.

When kids are young, most dirtbag rich parents harness their flexibility to spend more time at home rather than paying for daycare. Many make arrangements with other families, such as neighborhood playgroups or childcare cooperatives, that generate valuable social opportunities for parents and children alike.

As the kids get older, some parents send them to school like most everyone else. Others elect to homeschool, unschool, or worldschool. And yet others, like single mom **Victoria Bruce**, do something altogether more extreme, like hiking across New Zealand with her 7-year-old daughter for six months. Or there's **Ed Gillis**, who together with his wife took his three boys on multi-month cycle tours across Europe, Oceania, and Cuba on a shoestring budget. **Tracy and Andy Duncan** live full-time on a boat with their adopted teenage sons, who regularly socialize with other "boatschoolers" in the form of "roving pirate gangs." And **Daphné Robichaud** is partnered with a man who already has a child, which lets her simultaneously wear the hats of "seasonal outdoor guide" and "part-time mom."

Many people scratch their heads at the thought of raising children without a conventional home, job, or family constellation, but the frugality and open-mindedness of the dirtbag rich approach to life offers a powerful counterweight. Raising kids is never cheap or easy, but it also doesn't automatically require two full-time jobs and a white picket fence.

College tuition

There's no getting around this one: student debt is oppressive, and most dirtbag rich don't have to deal with it.

Some, like me, have their parents pay for college: a privilege, pure and simple.

Others, like **Artec Durham**, purposefully delay college until they know exactly what they want to study and can cobble together enough scholarships to escape debt-free. Artec lived out of his truck while climbing and working for NOLS for most of his twenties, took free community college classes in California, and just before turning 30, started nursing school at an affordable public university in Arizona that gave him multiple grants and was conveniently located next to incredible climbing.

Some bargain-hunters study abroad in countries with lower tuition. And some, like computer programmer **David Six**, never go to college at all, opting to educate themselves informally—and in David's case, also section-hiking the Pacific Crest Trail, Appalachian Trail, and Continental Divide Trail.

Eldercare

Do you need to earn bucketloads to care for your parents in old age? Fortunately for me, both of my parents are healthy and married to supportive partners and haven't yet required my assistance. If this weren't the case, my life might look different. But if a family member did require my assistance, my flexible life would help me take a supporting role—much like the itinerant adventurer **Diana Grijalva**, who explains:

> My grandpa died last winter, and I was able to fly home for the funeral and help my family empty out the house. When my uncle and aunt passed away, I could show up and just, like, be there. Living dirtbag rich makes it a lot easier to care for the people that you love, be responsible, and be supportive.

We like to assume that money can solve most problems. But even with a generous insurance policy or old-age benefits, the duty of caring for sick and infirm parents falls largely on their adult children. The more available you can be for those who matter most, in the moments they need you most, is a powerful form of wealth.

Pursuing a dream of dirtbag riches is always conditional on major factors outside of your control: the political system and economy, the fortune and misfortune of genetic inheritance, and family culture and obligations. However wild-west and ultra-individualist this dream may appear, it's still one rooted firmly in reality. Living this way may not be realistic, even when you seem made for it.

Do the best with the cards you're dealt, count your blessings, and when the rutted trail looks hopeless, search hard for the metaphorical side canyons.

CHOOSING TIME OVER MONEY IS A BLOODSPORT

ONCE YOU'VE DEVELOPED a skill that pays well, it can be difficult not to work and earn more—even when you're ultra-frugal.

Not long ago, it was the poor who worked the longest hours while the rich lounged, hunted, and painted.

Today, it's the rich who work the most extreme hours in response to the demands of "greedy jobs," a term popularized by economist Claudia Goldin to describe high-pay, high-responsibility positions that demand near-constant availability. (Think: finance, law, management consultants, and C-suite positions.)

No matter your income level, you're at risk of having all your time sucked up by work. Chalk it up to social media, scarcity-oriented monkey brains, the specter of "capitalism," or whatever else. Once you're capable of higher earnings, it's simply difficult to not exploit that power. It's not just about becoming self-employed or convincing your company to let you work part-time: deliberately earning less is an almost spiritual challenge that involves identity and self-worth.

Let's listen again to **Russell Max Simon**: the marketing consultant who worked for political nonprofits in Washington DC, transitioned to freelance work to avoid burnout, and ended up doing 15 hours a week of consulting in order to spend most of his time climbing, kitesurfing, dancing, and fixing up old houses.

Here's what Russell has to say about saying "no" to earning more money, despite social pressure and possessing the ability to do so:

> From the point of view of freedom, earning too little money is bad—but so is earning too much.
>
> When you build a business, you can take on any number of commitments. Maybe you take on investors; now you're beholden to your investors. Maybe you take on employees; now you have a responsibility to your employees. Maybe you go public; now you have regulatory responsibilities.
>
> Some of my clients are wealthy doctors. They run their own businesses, and they are extremely tied to responsibilities, whether they're on the board of some big medical organization or have professional standards to worry about.
>
> Having a bunch of money in the bank is not what restricts your freedom—it's the methods of getting that money, and the commitments they require, that limit your freedom.
>
> Ten years ago I was a marketing director within a company. I could have worked my way up the ladder, becoming a VP or Chief of Marketing. I could have done the same at the nonprofits or political organizations where I once worked. Instead, I walked away from these jobs. I became a freelance consultant. And once I had a few reliable long-term relationships, I stopped developing my business. I stopped trying to find new clients. Most importantly, I decided that I didn't want to expand my business to the point where I needed to hire someone. I didn't want to make someone else's

financial livelihood dependent on me.

When one of my big clients signed up for the newsletter where I started writing about my life, I thought, "Oh my God, what's this person going to think? They're going to read about me seeking meaning in other places. Will they even continue to give me their business?"

It turned out this person loved to surf and lived very far away from a surfing beach. They could only do it once or twice a year on family vacation. They envied the life that I had set up for myself. Once I realized that this was the most common reaction to my writing, I began to relax.

The more difficult thing has been explaining all this to my son, who grew up attending a school with other kids who have lots of money. He started looking around and wondering why I rented the smallest house in the neighborhood, why I drive a used Honda, and why I spend most of my time climbing. When he was eight, he started asking me, "Daddy, why don't you make more money? Why don't you go get more business?" And I had to explain to him over and over again, "I have enough money, kiddo. Do you see how much time I spend doing things I want to do? What would I do with more money?" And then he would say, "Well, buy a Tesla." And I'm like, "Yeah, those are cool. But I really like my Honda."

Even if I had a million dollars, I wouldn't spend a hundred thousand on a sports car. This is the main challenge I face: swimming against the cultural waves that makes my son question the idea that I really do feel wealthy, happy, and fulfilled with less money than all the other people in our neighborhood.

The cultural waves are strong, indeed. A big reason that John Maynard Keynes' 15-hour work week never materialized is that he discounted the effects of social comparison, a.k.a. "keeping up with the Joneses."

For many people, no amount of money can *ever* be enough as long as someone, somewhere, is making a *little bit* more money and having a *little bit* more fun.

That's why earning more money in less time isn't always the hardest part of becoming dirtbag rich. The real trick is learning to set limits, work less (even when your work is deeply meaningful), and not worry that someone, somewhere, might be having a bit more fun than you.

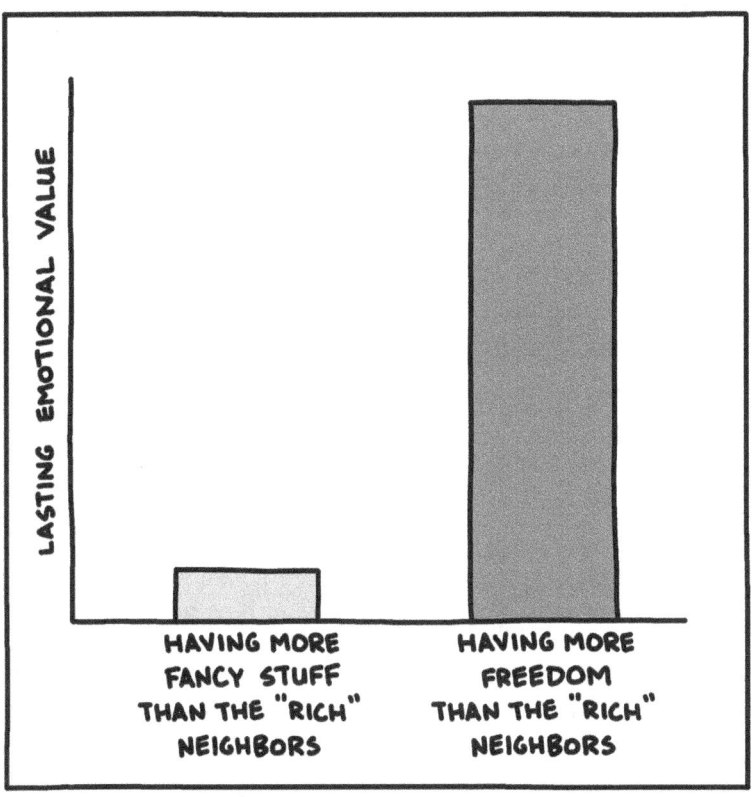

HOW TO KNOW IF YOU'RE WEALTHY

HOW DO YOU know when enough is enough?
In two decades of working with teenagers opting out of conventional education—and many who *want* to take this path but feel too scared or disoriented to make the leap—I've noticed a fascinating phenomenon. Accessing knowledge is not the biggest barrier to self-directed learning. It's about comparing yourself to others.

Many young people are aware that you can teach yourself almost anything by searching online or directly reaching out to people with specialized knowledge. But most never take the first step because they're not exactly sure where to start, how to navigate the wilderness, when they've arrived at their destination, or how to explain their learning journey to others. Most end up following the rutted path, because the rutted path offers clear goals (*getting a degree*), a clear method of social comparison (*grades and rankings*), and a validated path that no one will question (*school / college / grad school*).

It's the same for adults. Without a way to navigate the wilderness and know when you've "won," it's easy to regress to money, status, possessions, and retirement as your guiding lights.

Accruing a certain amount of material wealth *does* matter. Few people are capable of subsisting happily with no income or wealth whatsoever, like the wandering mystic Peace Pilgrim, the desert hermit Daniel Suelo, or the environmental activist Robin Greenfield.

But the "minimum" varies so wildly—based upon your personality, geography, health, goals, and family—that fixating on any particular number is a fool's game. You simply have no way of calculating how much money is "enough." (Distrust anyone who insists otherwise.)

Here are a few alternative ways to measure your wealth.

Depth & quality of relationships

As most people exit their twenties, build their careers, and start families, they lose their old friends and struggle to make new ones. Whether you've chosen a more domestic or freewheeling existence, ask yourself: can I avoid this fate? Time wealth isn't just about doing cool stuff in the outdoors by yourself; it's about giving yourself the flexibility and centeredness you need to invest in friends, family, activity partners, and romantic partners, rather than collapsing into a heap at the end of the day, week, or year. Invest more in a few individuals, or spread the love more widely; as long as your life choices result in a satisfying number of meaningful relationships, you are winning.

Nights slept under the stars

How many nights per year can you sneak away from civilization and invite moonlight to splash your face in the high country? This is just one such emotional-aesthetic metric; choose one that fits your own romantic ambitions. One summer, I was doing a lot of trail running in the mountains above Lake Tahoe. I devised a tracking system that recorded my route as well as my arbitrary assessment of its "beauty," my personal level of "stoke," and the "novelty" of the adventure as a whole. In other words, I was asking myself: How dramatic was the scenery, and how intense was the light? Was I feeling alive, challenged, delighted, bored? Was this a new path, an old favorite, or a sad slog? Rather than obsessing over distance, speed, performance, or FKTs (fastest known times)—another form of keeping up with the Joneses—I tracked my progress with metrics that actually mattered to me.

Good you've done in the world

This is a tricky one, because we all like to tell ourselves stories in which we're the heroes. But when you have a purpose-driven career, it's good to step back from time to time and reflect on what you've accomplished. For me, this means revisiting the emails I've tagged as "nice notes," where I accumulate the supportive messages that readers, parents, former students, and random people online have sent me about my writing, trips for teenagers, personal trip reports, and other public projects. Their words are deeply rewarding, and they help me remember that I'm not just screaming into the void.

Earning in one hour what you spend in one day

For the quantitatively minded, here's a metric. If you can earn in one hour what you typically spend in one day (inclusive of housing, taxes, and everything else), then you can work 15 hours a week while saving half your income. If, for example, you can earn $100/hour and spend $100 a day, you can earn $1500 per week while spending just $700 and saving $800. Reality is always messier than any equation, of course, but the overall idea holds. Maintain this kind of earning-to-spending ratio (or anything close to it), and your financial future is secure.

Historical perspective

Ask yourself, "How wealthy am I compared to a hundred, five hundred, or a thousand years ago?" Imagine you're in the same relative socioeconomic position as you are today. In all likelihood, you wouldn't be one of the very few people on top. You would have been a subsistence farmer with rotting gums, a factory worker with ruined lungs, a woman trapped in an arranged marriage, an enslaved person, or someone living in a closed society with rigid roles and few prospects for change. Even those on top of these societies were almost certainly less healthy and materially wealthy than you are today. Grasping all this requires a bit of reading in history and economics, but it's worth the investment. When you stop comparing yourself to those around you and start comparing yourself to the human experience writ large, it's hard to feel deprived.

"I could die now" moments

While writing this book, I attended a small dance event at a big house in Belgium. Of the 30 people in attendance, 20 were friends I'd made while dancing across Europe. It was a "co-created" weekend in which everyone offered something: a workshop, a DJ set, or in my case, two hours of summer-camp-style connection games. We cooked, cleaned, cuddled, napped, and danced together. I slept on a small mattress on my friend's floor. Somehow, everyone survived with just two toilets. The final evening ended with long hugs, an all-group folk dance, and an overflowing pile of Belgian fries.

Walking away Monday morning, my nervous system felt calm, and I found myself thinking: *This is really, truly, as good as it gets. If I got hit by a bus today, I could die happily.*

Why? Because I was caught in the act of fulfilling my purpose. Because despite the tragedy of an early death, I would have left this Earth doing what I'm supposed to do—feeling fully alive.

When such moments are common in life, you are truly dirtbag rich.

A DIRTBAG WITH A CAUSE

WHAT A TINGLING SPINE SAYS

AT AGE 19, I volunteered as a backcountry ranger in the Trinity Alps, an obscure mountain range in Northern California. I somehow landed the position despite having just one solo backpacking trip under my belt: an out-and-back jaunt in Sequoia National Park where I scrambled up a rocky ridge, munched on Corn Nuts and M&Ms, watched marmots raid my campsite from afar, and quietly told myself, *yes, I want more of this.*

At a Forest Service office, a kind-hearted senior ranger taught me how to check permits, drown campfires, and clear trail obstructions. Then he loaded me up with tortillas, granola bars, cheddar cheese, apples, and instant black beans, drove me up a long canyon, hiked with me for two days, gave me a high-powered radio, turned around, and promised to pick me up three days later.

It was early season. Hikers were few, my duties were light, and the weather was unstable. Storm clouds grew as I traversed the range, and on the third day, a long rain sent me into hiding. Curled up under my ultralight poncho-tarp, pitched teepee-style under a pine tree, I napped the afternoon away as a light drizzle soaked the foot of my sleeping bag.

I slept little that night: staring at the stars when clouds parted, changing my socks a few times, and contemplating what life had in store for me. I was alone, and I was pushing the edge of comfort and safety. But I could also feel the edge expanding.

Morning brought blue skies, seven easy miles to the trailhead, and one of the most curiously delightful moments of my young life.

Tramping down the canyon with a near-empty pack bouncing on my shoulders, surrounded by sun and breeze and birdsong, I became filled with a kind of effervescent joy. An electric tingling sensation ran up and down my spine, and an irrepressible grin plastered my face. I skipped, leaped, and twirled down the trail, occasionally bursting into laughter, marveling at the state of my otherwise sober mind. I remained in this giddy euphoria for what felt like a full hour.

Then I arrived at the trailhead, found the kind-hearted ranger, got into his truck—and the feeling evaporated.

But now I knew it existed.

In the adventures that lay ahead for me, the curious, spine-tingling sensation is one I would come to know well. It would symbolize many things: an expanding sense of self, a deepening confidence, a feeling of oneness with the natural world, and a joyous anticipation of returning to human society (as represented by showers, burritos, and the possibility of flirtation). The euphoria also found its way into my work life, appearing whenever I felt like I was making a genuine contribution to the world, like helping a 12-year-old learn to windsurf, leading a provocative conversation with a group of teenagers, or speaking with parents about the vibrant possibilities of life outside the school system.

The spine tingle became one of the main ways that I've determined whether my adult life is "on track"—if I'm doing what I'm meant to be doing and pursuing real wealth rather than mere security. It was a shimmering, bodily manifestation of something that all of us need and struggle to find.

SLIPPERIER THAN A CATFISH IN A VASELINE FIGHT

WHY IS THE SEARCH for purpose so complicated? Why must we voyage to obscure mountain ranges, far-flung countries, and the other strange and beautiful places of the world to taste even a hint of it?

Becoming dirtbag rich isn't only about thrift, time flexibility, or entrepreneurial savvy. These are means to an end. The ultimate goal of becoming dirtbag rich is to enjoy a truly deep sense of *purpose* or *meaning* in life.

Why does this matter?

For thousands of years, humans lived in tiny, ethnically homogenous enclaves with rigid gender roles and caste hierarchies. Young people began working early, married early, and had lots of children early, many of whom died early. Work was largely physical, religious belief was ubiquitous, and culture changed at a snail's pace. Most people found purpose through tradition and necessity, and however difficult and unfair life might have been, at least it was predictable. Then, in a few short centuries, everything changed.

To understand what drives the dirtbag rich, it helps to understand how human society has evolved. There are good reasons that people like us make the seemingly irrational (yet powerfully intuitive) choice to live differently. We're thirsty for purpose, and the usual wells have run dry.

Here are the largest changes wrought by modernity, as I understand them.

Work

One hundred and fifty years ago, half of adults worked in agriculture. Today, just two percent do. The industrial revolution brought factory work, globalization relocated it, and automation shrank it. The service sector bloomed, knowledge work became a thing, and the number of potential job titles exploded. Where once you might have known what your spouse, neighbors, friends, or children did for work, now you have little idea. This led some people to locate a deeper purpose in their new, specialized roles, but it left many others feeling alienated, disconnected, and cut off from work that is recognized and honored by others.

God and country

In just two short centuries, Darwin explained the origin of species, Nietzsche declared *God is dead*, and medicine began saving more lives than prayer. Mass secular education was born, the atrocities of two world wars shocked the collective consciousness, and down came the (already diminishing) belief in a loving creator. Alongside the decline in religion was the lessening of nationalist conviction—that age-old assumption that our homeland is *good* and *right* because we were born here. The energy that once coursed through political rallies and patriotic holidays now flowed into team sports, niche hobbies, and private enclaves. New forms of affordable transportation enabled friends and families to spread out, weakening traditional bonds to place. Rural life dwindled, cities flourished, communication technologies exploded, and people found themselves with more space, privacy, and loneliness than ever before.

Family

After untold centuries of enduring domestic gulags, women began escaping nightmarish home lives thanks to no-fault divorce laws. Effective birth control turned "family planning" into a reality. Widening cosmopolitan beliefs destigmatized "sexual deviancy" of all kinds. The nuclear family fissioned and released its energy into countless new constellations: same-sex marriages, chosen families, perpetual bachelors, DINKs (dual income, no kids), and polycules. Birth rates plummeted, individual children became more precious, and parenting evolved from a casual undertaking into a high-stakes pressure-cooker. The commandment to "get married and have kids" faded, and no other clear imperative rose to fill its shoes.

There's more to say, but here's the punchline: in a very short period of time (on the scale of human history), the once-unsinkable ships that once held us afloat have become unmoored. Our family structures, group allegiances, rigid identity boxes, geographic ties, and traditional sources of authority have largely disappeared. Purpose is no longer something we inherit but are forced to actively locate, and relocate, throughout life.

This is why the quest for purpose has become complicated, why it sends us to increasingly distant territories (interior and exterior), and why it's no longer confined to adolescence.

Once easily grasped, purpose is now a very slippery fish.

ECSTASY, TRANSCENDENCE, AND ADVENTURE

FAST-FORWARD 21 YEARS from the Trinity Alps: I'm a seasoned adult of 40. My eyes are closed, my smile is wide, and my arms are wrapped around my dance partner's body.

Together, we are moving to the music: spinning, tilting, pushing, pulling, rolling, shaking, gliding, pausing, stepping, dipping, and sometimes even twerking.

I'm in a large dance studio in Bern, Switzerland, in the middle of a 3-day fusion dance weekend. ("Fusion" brings together partner dancers from many different backgrounds, such as swing, salsa, tango, blues, kizomba, and contact improv.)

It doesn't matter who my specific dance partner is; I've had many throughout the weekend. About a quarter of the time, *she* is a *he*, or *they*, or *who knows, who cares?*

Body shape, gender, attractiveness, all are irrelevant. Instead, I pay attention to smile, warmth, enthusiasm, respect, responsiveness, and presence. The most important questions aren't: *Are we performing well?* or *Do we look good?* They are: *Can we listen to the music, find a connection, and create something beautiful? Can we pause our thinking and worrying? Can we play, transcend, and co-author ecstasy?*

Because that's why I'm here. Not to impress, not to win a competition, not to master a technique. I'm here to lose myself, and therefore find myself, over and over again. And you can bet my spine is tingling.

Dancing fusion in Europe, 2022

When the weekend is over, I will reflect on why, exactly, I am here: hopping from one gender-bending European dance weekend to the next, living out of a bicycle and a few bags rather than settled in my home country with a house, spouse, and children.

Is it Peter Pan syndrome, avoidant attachment, or an excess of romantic idealism? Why does the pursuit of ecstasy, transcendence, and adventure feel so much more real and pressing than the quest for security, status, and acceptance?

The answer I'll find is that I am neither special nor broken, but rather a product of a certain time, place, and cultural moment.

The answer is that people who pursue dirtbag riches do not operate in a cultural vacuum. We are the products of the intellectual movements that came before us—the slow-moving, centuries-long, global decline of purpose.

But we are also the products of a very specific, influential, and rapid movement that took place in a handful of countries within living memory.

We are heirs to the sixties.

GYRATING DIRTBAG FLOWER CHILDREN

JUST WHAT HAPPENED in the 1960s? As the philosopher Jules Evans tells the story,

Eastern contemplative practices, including Vipassana, yoga, tantra, Transcendental Meditation and Hare Krishna, were brought over to the West in the 1960s and attracted huge followings. New Age spirituality flourished through Wicca, magic, neo-shamanism, nature-worship and human potential encounter sessions. Psychedelic drugs became widely available. The sexual revolution encouraged people to search for the ultimate orgasm at swinger parties and leather clubs. People sought immersive experiences at art-happenings, experimental theatre and underground cinema. Rock and roll took Pentecostal ecstasy from black churches, secularised it, and brought it to white middle-class audiences. Even sport became a means to transcendence—people turned to surfing, mountain-climbing and jogging as a way to get out of their heads. There was a widespread urge to lose control, turn off the mind, find your authentic self, [and] seek intense experiences.

— *The Art of Losing Control* (2019)

It's no surprise that dirtbag culture arose during the sixties. As large numbers of middle-class people were seeking new kinds of purpose and widespread material prosperity was taking hold in the post-war period, the hardcore climbers of Yosemite Valley started using (and creating) newfangled equipment to undertake ever-more ambitious big wall projects. Amplified by new forms of mass media, their exploits inspired others, and soon enough, rock climbing had changed from a fringe pursuit to a mainstream sport (as did skiing, backpacking, surfing, running, sky-diving, and other activities once practiced by only a select few). Together, these countercultural adrenaline junkies and proto-dirtbags began authoring for themselves what they might have otherwise found, just a hundred years prior, at the pew, pub, or political rally: a profound sense of purpose, identity, and belonging.

The sixties were also a chaotic mess. As Jules Evans explains, the era's charismatic cult leaders, New Age nonsense, and drug-fueled excess brought new "compulsions, addictions, depressions, anxieties, and a constant sense of the artificiality and immorality of the civilisation in which we live," leading many to feel that life was "boring, depressing, atomised and meaningless." Never had so many people flirted so intensely with new modes of purpose, and the hangover was real.

In the 1970s, the pendulum of purpose swung back, and most of the intentional communities, back-to-the-land movements, and other radical experiments crumbled, making way for the more cautious, conservative, and corporate values of the eighties. But the pendulum swung again in the 1990s when the Cold War ended, the internet was born, an unprecedented optimism for global progress took hold, and a new type of counterculture was born: the "bohemian bourgeois." Socially progressive yet deeply money-oriented and careerist, the "bobos" successfully staked out a middle ground between the flower-child sixties and suit-and-tie eighties, showing the world that you can be both hip *and* rich. (Thus was born the "hipster.") The synthesis proved popular, and the bobo became the new aspirational standard for the middle classes of the WEIRD (Western, Educated, Industrialized, Rich, and Democratic) countries.

Thus did the countercultural spirit of the 1960s find its way into modernity, and I found myself bouncing down a trail with a tingling spine at age 19, running away to South America at 24, postponing "adulting" in my 30s, embracing strangers at dance weekends at 40, and otherwise seeking my "authentic self" through a never-ending series of intense outdoor, travel, inter- and intrapersonal experiences for two solid decades.

And such it was that you, dear reader, found your way to this book.

Two centuries of modernity have gifted you with a deep skepticism of traditional purpose. The 1960s cranked the volume. And more recent developments—like climate change, rapid globalization, and serial financial crises—delivered you to the doorstep of the life you're now leading, the choices you're now making, and the confusion you now feel about your purpose on this Earth.

There are additional reasons that some of us take the path I am both promoting (to you) and defending (to myself). Perhaps we are reacting to painful or disorganized upbringings by attaching ourselves to seemingly pure entities (like wilderness) that won't betray us. Perhaps we glorify thrift because we are genuinely incapable of earning more than our parents or cannot bear the thought of making the same trade-offs they made. Perhaps our obsession with physical activity masks our eating disorders, body image issues, or a need to feel superior. Perhaps there's some seriously atypical neurology baked into our cakes.

Perhaps we delay or reject parenthood because we fear the costs, consequences, and culture of bringing children into the world, and we haven't found many role models worth emulating. Perhaps we continue our endless migrations because we don't like who we become when we're stationary, because we wish to avoid the uglier, harder, and boring sides of life, or because we don't want to be forced to witness the world's profound sameness, illness, and sadness.

Almost certainly, much of this is outside our control.

Zoom out far enough, and these are the uncharted edges of our map. Like the seekers who came before us, we are reconnoitering new territory, unsure of which dragons lay beyond.

Why do we gyrate in perpetual motion, empty our minds in feats of endurance, lose ourselves in blissed-out reverie, and seek our centers again in wilderness solitude? It is not because we are noble or enlightened. Rather it is due to a unique combination of time, place, culture, and circumstance. We are privileged and dissatisfied, a herd of individualists, and a mess of contradictions.

But everyone searches for purpose. This is our search. On we go.

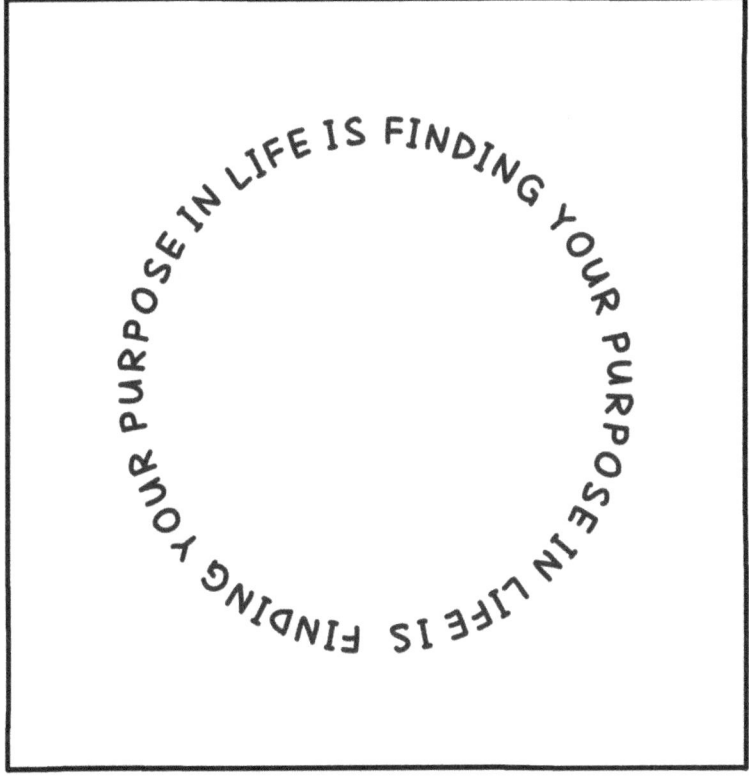

DRINKING FOUNTAINS OF MEANING

TO SLAKE OUR eternal thirst for meaning, the dirtbag rich drink from four fountains:

Our cherished physical activities

Our epic mountain runs, meandering cycle trips, afternoon microadventures, late-night dances, cross-country jaunts, and other moments of motion, balance, flight, pain, sweat, and ecstasy. Here we find our tingling spines, irrepressible grins, life-enhancing fitness, and delicious cocktails of brain chemicals.

Our close relationships

Just like normal people, we hold our friends, family, and professional colleagues close. But they are not our entire worlds. For we also revere our adventure partners, travel buddies, housemates, mentors, collaborators, and other characters who enter our lives—as well as the landscapes where these connections occur. Collectively held, all are "close relationships," and they are why we obsess over our festivals, gatherings, missions, races, retreats, and solitudes. These relationships are our *raison d'être*, and they are the nets that catch us when we fall.

Our purposeful work

The dirtbag rich do not fear or begrudge the work that funds our lives, because our work is an end in itself. Some parents will fret that we're earning "less than we could." But if moral alignment and mental health are also currencies, then loved ones can rest assured we are absolutely maximizing our earning potential.

Our freedom

Above all else, the dirtbag rich prize freedom. Without it, we cannot lustily pursue our ridiculous dreams, cannot congregate with our favorite people, and cannot earn our money in our own, strange, bespoke ways. Whatever this word "freedom" means to us, it is as necessary as air and water.

If you wish to become (and remain) dirtbag rich, you need to drink regularly from these four fountains. Do this, and life will be good. Forsake any fountain for too long, and you will find yourself clawing belly-down through the scorched desert of boredom, depression, atomization, and meaninglessness.

Let's consider each fountain in turn.

THE CHURCH OF THE WILD

WHAT'S BETTER THAN GOD? Ultrarunning. When **Tim and Angel Mathis** met and married in college, both were devout Christians. Then they traveled to Australia, lived abroad amid the natural splendor of New Zealand for a couple of years, and met all sorts of people from outside the bubbles in which they were raised. Returning to settle in the Pacific Northwest, Tim did youth work in churches for 5 years, and then pivoted to join Angel as a nurse at age 30.

Tim and Angel were already questioning the central role of religious faith in their lives. Fortuitously, as they felt a need to step back from Christianity, they were able to find new purpose through trail running, long-distance hiking, open water paddling, and other forms of intense outdoor recreation. Park runs began to replace prayer groups, races started to feel like revivals, and Sundays no longer meant church but epic, day-long adventures. Together, the couple would go on to thru-hike the Pacific Crest Trail, run the Camino de Santiago, and participate in multiple ultramarathons.

For Angel, "finding the outdoors felt good because it took over the rituals and traditions that church once gave me." For Tim, "the long hikes and runs provided a structure and a lot of really positive feelings, at a time when I was having a lot of negative feelings"—abandoning his long-held dream of becoming an Episcopal minister accompanied by the sudden loss of his father to an aggressive form of cancer in the middle of the Pacific Crest Trail adventure. But through his relationship to wilderness and various outdoor communities, Tim discovered the solace he needed to move forward. Leaving the Christian faith meant losing many friends and a large support network, but in exchange, Tim and Angel discovered a deep fountain of purpose that fit them much better.

Alastair Humphreys also grew up traditionally Christian in the United Kingdom, and he maintained his faith throughout university. Then he set off to cycle around the world—a shoestring adventure that ended up lasting four years and kept him constantly immersed in the outdoors and foreign cultures. What Alastair calls his own version of "40 days in the wilderness" ended up transforming him profoundly in ways that diminished, rather than reinforced, his Christian faith:

> I spent a lot of time in Muslim, Buddhist, Shinto, and other parts of the world. I saw no evidence of any higher powers. When I came home, I asked myself, "How can I choose the Christian team rather than, say, the Muslim or Buddhist team? Why does this not seem right?" I lost any semblance of faith. Now I'm an atheist who is filled with awe and wonder and very interested in grace and mystery.
>
> I still love churches, mosques, and other places like that. Whenever I'm out exploring my local map and there's a little village church, I love going in and sitting there. I very much enjoy these spiritual places. But I'm not a spiritual person anymore.

Two decades later, Alastair is married with two children. Instead of getting high on the epic adventures that defined his life for many years—like rowing across the Atlantic ocean or crossing the Arabic Empty Quarter on foot—he now microdoses adventure in a nondescript corner of England: sleeping on hilltops, jumping into rivers, walking places where one is not supposed to walk, and exploring new areas by bicycle, sometimes with kids in tow, whenever he can.

Where Jesus once held an important place in Alastair's heart, now the most important thing is adventure. Alastair even built a career out of evangelizing on its behalf: speaking for schools and businesses, writing books and newsletters, and publishing videos about why adventure matters and how to get started, regardless of one's age, place, or fitness level. He preaches adventure, practices it, and believes it can lead us toward a good and purpose-filled life.

Just a few hundred years ago, people like Angel, Tim, Alastair, and perhaps even me would have given our whole hearts to Jesus, Mohammed, Yahweh, the Buddha, or another figure at the center of a powerful system of organized religious belief. Today, we're more likely to give our hearts to wilderness, travel, adventure, and endurance sports. We prostrate before granite massifs, commune with silent forests, pilgrimage to sacred destinations, minister to our adventure partners, pray for healthy knees and deep powder, and seek moments of effortless flow and transcendent union with nameless entities beyond ourselves. Some of us maintain our traditional religious beliefs; many others downgrade, alter, or merge them with our love of nature.

I myself was raised ultralight-Christian (borderline agnostic), shaped more by California consumerism than anything pitched by Jesus. Then came wilderness summer camp at age 11, living in Chile with a host family at 14, a handful of ecstasy-inducing snowboard carves in British Columbia at 18, and the spine-tingling revelation in the Trinity Alps at 19. By that point, I was sold. Take my money, my time, my life, oh God of the Wild, oh Deity of Travel, oh Lord of Adventure, for there is nothing better than you!

All the adventures to come—all the backpacking trips, trail runs, scree scrambles, cycle tours, slacklining and acroyoga and roadtrips and sweaty nights of dancing—all would trace back to these formative moments when I decided to locate my higher power *here* and *now*, among the rock, sun, trees, dirt, lakes, highways, foreign lands, and communities of fellow nature- and movement-worshippers.

All I wanted was a bit of purpose, and if possible, a healthy dose of awe, rapture, reverence, wonder, humility, union, and satori. God did not grant this to me, so I looked elsewhere—and I found it.

I'll see you at church.

A DIVERSIFIED RELATIONSHIP PORTFOLIO

"**I'M 40,** and I'm single," mountain athlete **Jenny Abegg** told me:

> The idea of building a life with someone and starting a family feels like it's slowly drifting away. This is something I've spent a lot of time grieving.
>
> At the same time, I'm very content to be single. The freedom is golden. It makes me feel alive.
>
> Still, I can't help thinking that I'm missing out on something that a lot of humans get to experience: the level of connection that you get when you are partnered.

We commitment-phobes, we hyperindividualists, we perpetual bachelors and bachelorettes—what's wrong with us? Does our endless craving for flexibility and freedom destine us to die alone in our vehicles, parked along some desolate highway, mummified in our sleeping bags?

Some friends and family may quietly suspect this. *You* may quietly suspect this. But what I've witnessed is that the dirtbag rich do prioritize relationships—we just think about them differently.

While most people typically invest in a handful of childhood friends, family members, and romantic partners, the dirtbag rich tend to spread their investments more widely.

Instead of going all-in on a few stocks, we're the owners of highly diversified relationship portfolios.

First, we love the wild and foreign places of the world: the mountains, deserts, canyons, coastlines, and distant lands that we know so well, our dirt-encrusted cathedrals.

I am in a very serious, long-term relationship with a particular valley just outside South Lake Tahoe, one where I've experienced profound thoughts and feelings over 15 years of running, hiking, and meandering. This connection does not offer the depth or responsiveness of a human—trees cannot hug you back—but it is a relationship nonetheless. Every time I'm near South Lake Tahoe, my heart demands that I provide devoted attention to this valley and its crunching pine needles, strewn granite boulders, and cold, rushing winds. I know it's love, because losing it would hurt.

Second, we dirtbag rich fall in love with our communities as much as we do with individuals.

The two youth camps where I served for many summers—one centered on wilderness, the other on unschooling—showed me how temporary, intensive communities can become combustion chambers of growth, connection, and love.

At the wilderness camp, we practiced a culture of extreme positivity, contribution, and endurance. At the unschooling camp, we practiced intentional inclusiveness, warmth, and self-reflection. Working at these camps back-to-back for multiple years felt like a dual partnership with very different lovers. One encouraged me to become a gladiator, an explorer, and a world-builder. The other encouraged me to become a nurturer, a clown, and a deep listener. When I eventually set out to create my own community—the traveling programs for unschoolers—I borrowed from both lineages. Such is love transmitted. The friends I made at those camps remain some of my closest and most durable, alloys forged in the furnace of community.

Justin Riley is no stranger to the life-shaping power of activity-oriented communities. As a long-time organizer of outdoor fusion dance weekends, he's seen what such gatherings can offer:

> I've had more people than I can count tell me that these spaces have saved their lives in a very material way. They were feeling lost and suicidal, and then they found the dance community. I don't think I'm the one doing this, of course. It's all these people coming together, crashing into each other in these poetic ways, eating good food, being in nature, falling in love, and treating each other better than we would in the outside world.

A community worthy of love isn't just an accident of geography—it's a declaration of shared values and mutual obsession. The communities that form around climbing, long-distance hiking, river running, backcountry skiing, downhill mountain biking, long-term world travel, highlining, ultrarunning, acroyoga, partner dance, and Burning Man-style gatherings are immersive, transformative, and borderline cultish. You spend intense time around others. Personal boundaries come down. Habits, characters, and neuroses are revealed. Human connections form quickly and deeply. The climbing, skiing, or hiking may bring you into the dirtbag life, but it's the community that hooks you.

Finally, the dirtbag rich *do* make long-term romantic commitments. Many of my interview subjects are durably partnered or married. Some are happy parents, like **Julieta Duvall**, **Ed Gillis**, **Kelsey Shipman**, and **Alastair Humphreys**. Some are contentedly childfree, like **Suzanne Roberts**, **David Six**, **Courtney Bierschbach**, and **Tim and Angel Mathis**. The myth of the lonely elder dirtbag, the wanderer who could never settle, the commitment-phobic nomad, may be just that—a myth.

Committed relationships aren't incompatible with a dirtbag's love of constant exploration, physical activity, and community participation—as long as your partner accepts that, even when devoutly monogamous, your love is not theirs alone. For we dirtbag rich are polyamorous in the broadest sense of the word: we are enamored with many peoples, many places, and many ways of moving through this world.

We struggle to find domestic bliss in a single geography and among one narrow slice of humanity. We've made friends in many places whom we prefer not to abandon. Many of our loves do not, will not, and cannot involve our partners. Our connections are multitude, our horizons are vast, and our lips are stained with the juices of many fruits.

Most of us *do* wish to be partnered. We *do* want someone to join some of our adventures, to give us space to take our own adventures, and hopefully take some of their own. But if we don't end up in such a relationship, it's not the end of the world. By having many sources of love and connection, committed partnership becomes more of a choice and less of a desperate need.

"I don't think my lifestyle is the reason why I'm not partnered," **Jenny Abegg** told me:

> There are many answers to that question: my religious upbringing, attachment stuff, and also just loving my independence. Therapy helped me realize that there are no "shoulds"—like the idea that I'm 40 and should be married and having kids. I can throw that out the window because what I'm doing now is working for me, and it feels good. What doesn't feel good is comparing myself to others.

Without a capital-R relationship, a dirtbag life can still be rich. Being single is a gateway into deeper dedication to friends, family, and other people's children. It makes space for our cherished places, communities, and worldly contributions. Added up, such a relationship portfolio pays impressive dividends. It doesn't fit the standard mold that well-meaning friends and family may want for us. But if you already think differently about work, time, and money, why not love, too?

ANTI-BULLSHIT JOBS

PURSUING YOUR FAVORITE activities, being outdoors frequently, and nurturing good relationships is a strong foundation for a purposeful life. But if you support this life with morally questionable employment, then your dirtbag riches will be tainted.

Here are a few questions you can ask to assess the purposefulness of your own work, and if necessary, begin correcting course.

Do you possess reliable evidence that your work is improving the lives of real people? As the anthropologist David Graeber famously observed, "shit jobs" may be unpleasant but important—like garbage collectors—while "bullshit jobs" are respected and well-paid but ultimately pointless, like many corporate lawyers, public relations consultants, telemarketers, brand managers, and administrative specialists. If you have to do mental gymnastics to justify the existence of your position, there's a good chance it's bullshit.

Former corporate consultant **Paul Millerd** knows this feeling well:

> In one of my jobs, I would have just five to ten hours of client work a week, but I was still expected to commute and be in the office for more than 55 hours a week. I literally did laps around the office, drank extra coffee just to feel something, and took two-hour lunches in the park, sometimes napping on the grass. That might

sound like "getting away with doing nothing," but to me it was worse than being busy because I was constantly aware of the fact that I was not free.

Does your work contribute to the reduction of socially sanctioned cruelty? For me, the all-too-common experiences of classroom boredom, bullying, and wasted time represent a form of cruelty that far too many people accept as normal. I believe that future generations will look back upon our mass education system as barbaric, much as we now view child factory labor in the 1800s. By writing about, speaking about, and creating alternatives to school that seem genuinely positive for young people, I believe I'm contributing to a small but important reduction in the world's total cruelty.

That's my great big social concern—what's yours? That old people should not be locked away from society? That animals should not be grown only for slaughter? That certain drugs should not be banned from clinical research? That other kinds of energy production deserve a chance? That we should get more city kids into the woods? That basic communication skills can solve a huge number of problems?

In his 2025 book *Moral Ambition*, the Dutch historian Rutger Bregman offers a clear-eyed summary of our current situation:

1. The world's in awful shape. There's untold suffering among billions of people and animals.
2. The world's much better off than three centuries ago. We are healthier and wealthier than ever.
3. The world can be a wildly better place. Just look at how much money and talent we're still wasting.
4. The world has never been closer to its own demise.

These factors point to some pretty unambiguous takeaways. You don't need grandiose ambitions to have purposeful work. You just need to *clearly* help someone and *clearly* do less harm than good. You might improve systems in rich countries or poor countries, or might work directly with more advantaged or less advantaged people. You are not required to dedicate your life to serving the most downtrodden; idealistic burnout is a real thing. Consider problems you genuinely care about and find ways to contribute to improving them. It's better to do something rather than nothing.

The one thing you shouldn't say, if your goal is dirtbag riches rather than mere hedonism, is this: *I'll just do whatever I'm good at, pays well, and supports my hobbies.* This is how otherwise intelligent people end up selling sugar water, defiling wild places, building murderous robots, and creating ever-more intrusive forms of advertising.

It's challenging to find work that checks all the boxes: doing good, paying well, and staying flexible. This is why most of the dirtbag rich end up working for themselves. Most traditional jobs simply demand too much sacrifice in terms of time and purpose.

(Caveat: exceptions abound! Whitewater guide **Michael Hughes** enjoys a meaningful, seasonal livelihood working for a rafting company in Oregon. Speech therapist **Hannah Bowley** adores her otherwise normal job with Seattle Public Schools, the one that lets her take one year off after every three. And flight attendant **Julieta Duvall** builds her schedule fresh each month, enabling time for personal and family adventures.)

Sticking with normal jobs for a while may be necessary to build the skills, confidence, and connections necessary to branch out on your own. But remember that, for people like us, such jobs are usually lily pads, not landing strips. Get in, get what you need, get out, and then get on with making your unique contribution to the world: anything that energizes you, feels important, doesn't monopolize your life, and hasn't the slightest odor of bullshit.

FREEDOM FROM AND FREEDOM TO

THE FINAL DRINKING fountain of meaning is this thing we call *freedom*: something over which every member of the dirtbag rich obsesses, even if they cannot precisely define it. We're not just talking about the basic political freedoms of movement, association, speech, and equal treatment under the law. We're talking about something that we might better label *agency*, *optionality*, or what the expat relationship counselor **Peter Kowalke** calls an *infinite runway*. It's what many people assume money can buy, yet something that many monetarily wealthy people still lack.

But the best lens through which to look may be the age-old distinction between *freedom from* and *freedom to*. Two of my first dirtbag rich interview subjects, who lead two quite different lives, offer a window into this distinction.

Brittany Goris has neither a permanent homebase nor a long-term relationship—but she does possess a boundless sense of freedom.

For Brittany, life truly began when she stopped trying to adapt to city life, moved into her vehicle, took a part-time graphic design position (with a socially meaningful cause), and started climbing nearly every day. Brittany became a deeply independent world-wanderer who is also deeply embedded in her climbing community:

> Stability doesn't really hold a whole lot of value to me compared to freedom. I just have this ability to do whatever I want, without being tied down by the constraints of living in one place. Everything that happened before I started living this way just feels like a prologue.
>
> Let's say I'm in my van and I go to Indian Creek, the climbing mecca near Moab, Utah. I'm in this campground with all of these amazing people. There's no cell service. We climb together all day. We share all these emotional moments. And then we make dinner together, sit around a campfire, wake up the next day, and do it all again.
>
> That's not how life looks every single day, but it's a core example of how I build connections. I get to spend all of my time in these beautiful places around people that inspire me. It creates such an incredible sense of belonging. Yet I still have the freedom to go where I want, as does everyone else. It just all works together harmoniously.

Brittany enjoys two types of freedom: *freedom from* the constraints of her previous urban existence, and *freedom to* associate with her chosen family of fellow dirtbags among the cliffs and canyons of the American West. Her experience is captured well by the writer Maggie Nelson:

> Some people do not find—indeed, cannot find—refuge where others imagine they could or should find it; some forgo anchors for lines of flight; some instinctively spurn moralistic edicts set forth by others; some find—or are forced to find—solace or sustenance in nomadism, cosmic hoboism, unpredictable or uncouth identifications, illegible acts of disobedience, homelessness, or exile than in a place called Home.
>
> — *On Freedom* (2021)

Brendan Leonard lived like Brittany for a number of years, and then he got married, bought a house, and had a kid. He now faces considerably more constraints than his previously freewheeling dirtbag existence, yet he still considers himself dirtbag rich:

> For me, being a dirtbag is about freedom. Not in the "American manspreading" sense, where my right to do whatever I want trumps your rights, and I don't have to consider your feelings. More like: the freedom to do generally what I want with my day, or with my life.
>
> Here's an example. I wake up, and after my wife or I bike our son, Jay, to daycare, I've got eight hours. Most of this time is governed by deadlines for the next thing I need to get done, so it's not stress-free. But to a pretty big extent, I can pretty much do whatever I want, provided that it somehow leads to money or serves another purpose. Some days I drop Jay off and then ride our ridiculous cargo bike over to a trailhead. I run up a local mountain, run down, and bike home. I get home around 10:45, and then I start working.
>
> I was born an anxiety-ridden person. I'm constantly like, "Oh God, I gotta get this thing done by the end of the week!" But in the big picture, I'm doing less and less stuff that I don't want to do for money. Running my own business is actually pretty fun. I can be generous if I want, I can pinch pennies, I can ask people for money, or whatever—it's largely up to you.
>
> We can have Jay in daycare just four days a week instead of five because my wife and I don't necessarily have to work on Fridays. We get to have him at home and watch him grow up and learn to be a human being. That's pretty amazing.

We could have a nicer house, nicer cars, or less drafty doors. We probably need to upgrade the boiler. Do I ever think about getting a real job? Probably like three or four times a week. But here I am, still doing my own thing. Once you've tasted this amount of freedom, it's hard to go back.

Brendan enjoys the *freedom to* spend more time with his young child, earn money in his own way, and take long runs in the mountains. He enjoys *freedom from* a schedule that doesn't match his personality and daily rhythms. He still has profound obligations and a certain degree of stress and anxiety. But like Brittany, he gets to wake up every day and fit together the puzzle pieces, over and over again, creating a life that includes endless amounts of the people, places, and kind of work he loves most.

Whether you're rooted or wandering, married or single, traditionally employed or self-employed, high net worth or low net worth, the dirtbag rich quest for purpose boils down to this: Is your life filled with more "I have to" statements, or more "I get to?"

The first reveals a lack of freedom. The second reveals an abundance.

This is the pool into which all other fountains empty, and the same pool that reflects the proper definition of *progress*. When an increasing number of people lead lives of *I get to* instead of *I have to*—when more of us, everywhere, enjoy both *freedom from* and *freedom to*—then the world is genuinely improving.

This is the driving force behind the centuries-long reevaluation of "purpose." This is what the cultural innovators of the 1960s attempted to bring about, in their own flawed ways. And this is why pursuing dirtbag riches is nothing to be ashamed of, as long as you somehow improve the world along the way.

You are participating in a long, slow, and honorable tradition: the expansion, retooling, and fine-tuning of human freedom.

You may not sense this when you're tramping down a sodden trail, dancing all night with beautiful strangers, or perched around a campfire with friends made just months ago, but you are part of something bigger. And as long as you continue mustering the courage to live differently—not for the sake of being different, but for the vibrant energy, optimism, and pro-social spirit that living this way engenders—then you can keep doing this for a long, long time.

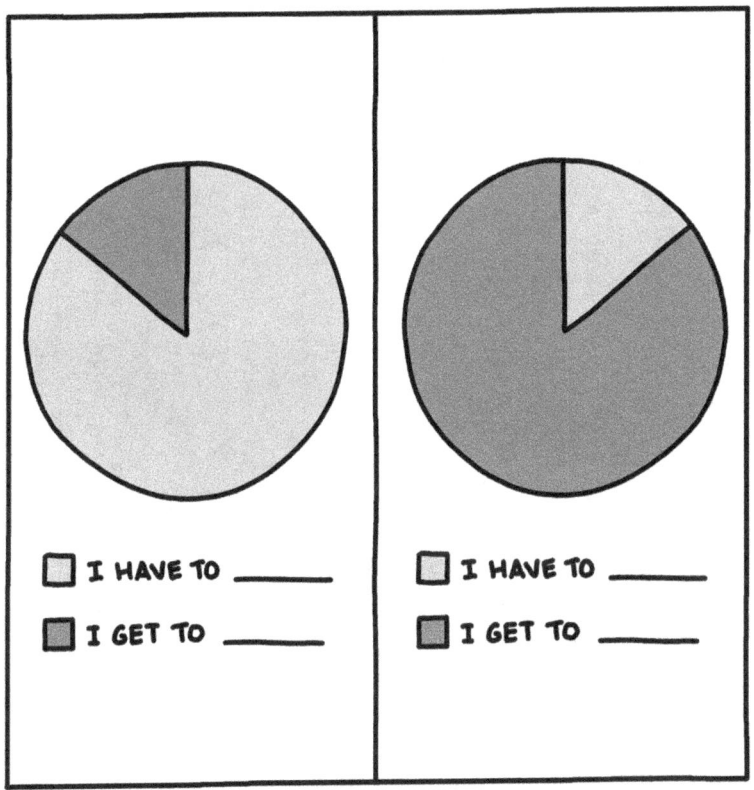

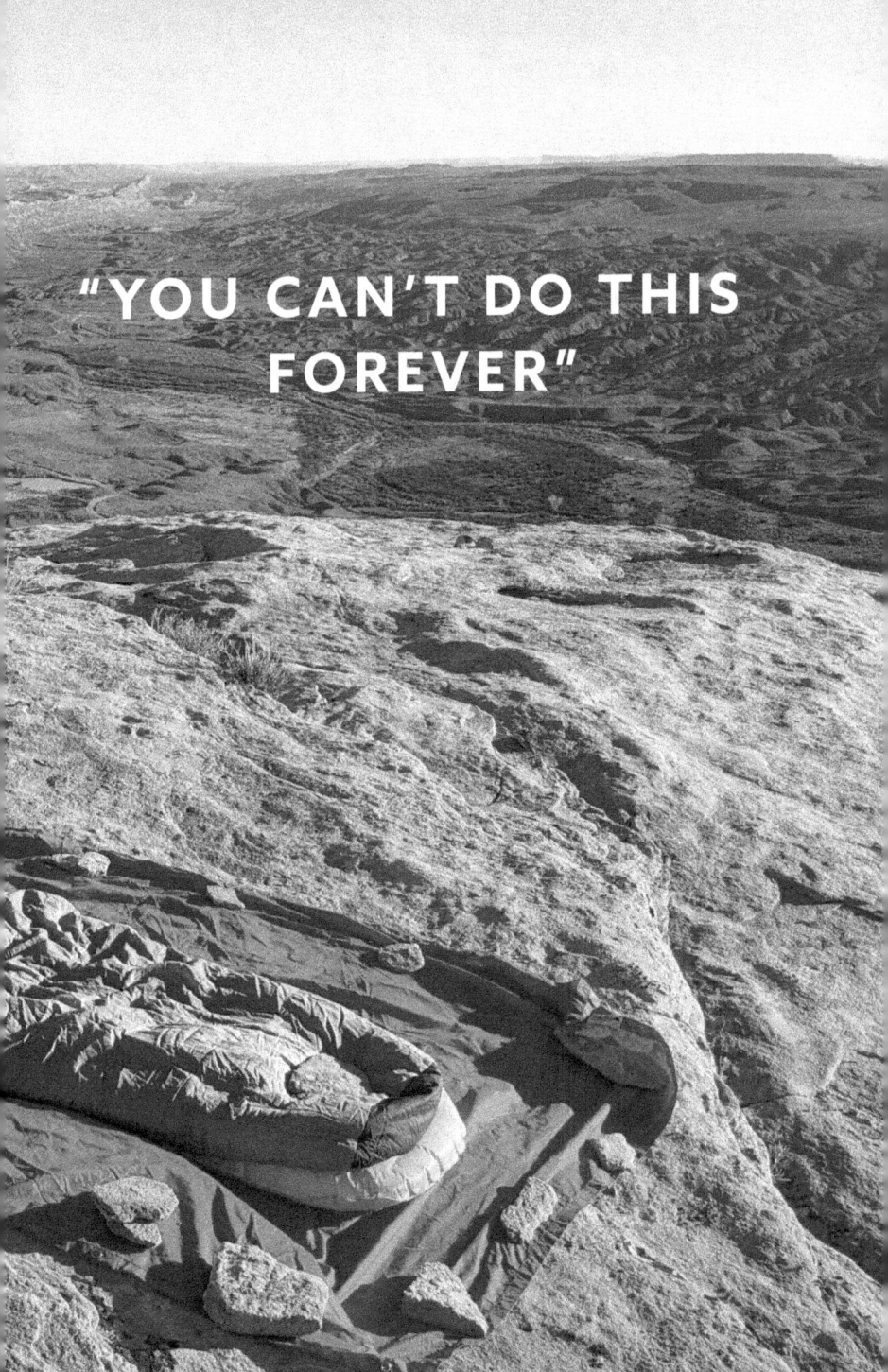

WALKING THE HIGHLINE

HIKING UP to Yosemite Falls one sunny spring morning, I saw a body dancing in the air.
Is it who I hope?
Yes—a slackliner.

Not just any slackliner, but a highliner: a daredevil floating, bobbing, and inching along a taut ribbon while suspended above the void, secured by little more than a harness and a few trailing carabiners.

Roaring with snowmelt, the falls pumped towering mists into the air that wheeled, twisted, and engulfed the walker, who proceeded with utmost concentration, face flashing between angelic joy, concerned calculation, and barely contained terror.

"I'd love to do that. I *will* do that," I told myself.

Later that day, I added two entries to my life goal list:

- Walk a 100-foot slackline.
- Walk a highline.

I had slacklined casually for more than a decade, messing around on short, 20- to 30-foot lines between trees in public parks. Now I purchased a 100-foot line, determined to see how much farther I could go.

Not much farther, it turned out.

Something funny happens when a slackline extends beyond 50 feet:

the swings become violent, the vertical brings vertigo, and mounting the line requires circus-level acrobatics.

Every time I tried walking a longer line—even someone else's professional rig, rather than my homebrew setup—it ejected me, deftly and conclusively.

Perhaps I wasn't light or lithe enough. Perhaps I didn't put in the hours necessary to develop the balance. Or perhaps this simply wasn't a dream I was fated to achieve.

I still haven't walked a highline, and I may never.

But at the same moment I found the misty highliners above Yosemite Falls, a different adventure was unfolding: I was collaborating with a family in California to fulfill my long-held dream of starting a seasonal boarding school for self-directed teenagers. (Project codename: *Hogwarts for Unschoolers*.)

Two of the family's daughters had attended my international trips, and following a financial windfall, the mom wanted to make an idealistic business investment that could involve her kids. She'd heard me speak at a homeschool conference, became familiar with my dream of starting a boarding school, and reached out to me. Following a few months of mutual vetting, I helped the family conduct a nationwide property search, resulting in their purchase of a beautiful piece of land in the California foothills, not far from Yosemite.

That spring, they had begun breaking ground on the construction of a large central building which would later be surrounded by an assembly of tents, yurts, and tiny houses. I'd flown out to help organize a work retreat on the property, building tent platforms and breaking trails with the assistance of the daughters and a few other teenagers they'd met on my trips. The hike to Yosemite Falls was a fun, final outing to say "thank you" to these young volunteers.

Almost out of a storybook, my dream of starting a residential, nature-based alternative school seemed to be coming true.

Then, seemingly out of nowhere, the collaboration was canceled. The family decided they lacked the energy for such a project and preferred to keep the property for their own purposes. After a year of careful co-creation, it was over. There would be no school.

I remained on friendly terms with the family, but the whole episode taught me a lesson about the nature of power: it's better to be free, independent, and sustained by smaller, relatively equal relationships, rather than investing in one giant, asymmetrical relationship.

I still haven't started a boarding school, and I may never.

Much like walking a slackline, building a dirtbag rich life requires careful attention, frequent adjustment, and preparation for sudden ejection at any moment.

Merely standing on a slackline is difficult. (Analogy: starting your own business or freelance career.)

Walking a short line without holding someone's hand is an unachievable feat for many. (Analogy: paying your bills without working full-time, while also saving money).

And from there, the lines only get longer, taller, and scarier. (Analogy: doing this year after year, even as your friends "move on" to other stages of life.)

To live dirtbag rich for more than a brief period—to enjoy plentiful time, money, and purpose over the long haul—is a highline of epic proportions. You're tracing a wobbly strip of one-inch nylon webbing across a windy, gaping chasm.

Ideally, you're attached to a bombproof leash: your friends, communities, health, savings, and ability to learn, pivot, and reinvent yourself.

But even with a leash, falling in the middle of a highline is no joke. It's a long, scary, and potentially exhausting bail out to solid ground, crawling hand-over-hand through the void. It's also humbling, and perhaps humiliating: a vivid declaration to the observers below that you aimed too high, couldn't hang, and might not be cut out for this kind of thing.

The novelist Verlyn Klinkenborg once described writing as *a perpetual act of self-authorization*. The same goes for living dirtbag rich. No one will anoint you. No school counselor, career coach, or family member will ever sit you down and say, "Have you considered living this way?"

Instead, you will be out on a (metaphorical) hike one day, and you will witness an act of daring and beauty. You'll see someone attempting the seemingly insane—yet when you meet this person, they won't appear unhinged. They'll feel alive. And when you ask them how they achieved this feat, the answer will always be some version of this: *a perpetual act of self-authorization.*

Few people walk highlines. You need the right combination of culture, personality, mentors, and resources. But even with those, most people choose a life closer to the ground. They do not authorize themselves. The fear of falling, and being *seen* falling, is too great.

I did not walk a highline. I did not start a school. But I gave myself permission to try. That was the reward, and that was the point.

If you've made it this far, you're clearly no stranger to self-authorization.

But you might be wondering: how far does this line go? How long can I walk among the mist and granite? How long can I authorize myself to live so differently?

Ropes fray and bodies decay. What's the endgame here?

A DIRTBAG RETIREMENT PLAN

IF YOU PRIORITIZE travel, freedom, and adventure beyond a brief period in your twenties, are you setting yourself up for destitution in old age? Will you end up in some horrible, state-funded nursing home? Will you hang your head in shame when you must ask friends or family for a loan, handout, or place to stay?

These fears are real—and they are potentially limitless.

You can always spend more time "planning for your future." You can always do a better job of "setting yourself up."

How much money do you need for a secure retirement? A million dollars? Two million? More? Better put that nose to the grindstone!

I don't wish to make light of such anxieties, but I also don't want to indulge them. Nor do I believe that hailing from a middle- or upper-class background automatically nullifies such concerns. (It can just as easily amplify them.)

Here are the biggest reasons I believe that the dirtbag rich path—one that explicitly *does not* optimize for wealth in old age—will nevertheless lead to a secure future:

- You solidify the habit of living below your means and maintaining a high savings rate. Even if that doesn't result in a massive pile of money, it's an infinitely sustainable way to live, and one that

always leaves you *something* to fall back on.
- Your time flexibility allows you to invest heavily in personal relationships and personal health: two "assets" extremely useful for weathering (and avoiding) the catastrophes that strike later in life. (An older person with poor health and few friends is a fragile creature, indeed.)
- Your entrepreneurial experiences train you to stay alert to situations where you might assist, innovate, or otherwise be of service: traits that other human beings *always* notice, value, and reward.

Should you plan to spend more money on healthcare later in life? Yes, of course. Don't let that fact become a bludgeoning tool that smashes all creative risk-taking. And remember: if your income remains lower than average, you are probably entitled to cheap (or free) state-subsidized policies. Thank your lucky stars, and your high-earning neighbors, for that one.

What about the end of life? Wouldn't it be nice to sit in a rocking chair on the front porch of the spacious, beautiful home that you own outright? Yes, of course—but at what cost?

As we've seen, the dirtbag rich path *can* involve homeownership. I myself envision joining (or creating) a mutual-aid living arrangement with other hobbled dirtbags, ex-dancers with bad hips, and hippie co-housing types.

Can I point to any such hip, alternative retirement communes that exist today? No, I cannot. Can I point to many older people who spent their lives working full-time, in jobs they don't particularly care about, and now enjoy a basically secure retirement in their private castles? Yes, I can. Does this scare me? No, it doesn't.

In my more cavalier moments, I'll tell you that my retirement plan is to die penniless and beloved. Maybe I'll permanently pilgrimage the Camino de Santiago or bike around the world till my tires pop and my heart stops. Maybe I'll become "that old guy" in the mountain town: a mysterious wispy-haired geriatric who hangs around coffee shops, volunteers at libraries, and has a hundred good stories to tell.

We simply don't know what's going to happen later in life. This fact can lead you to an infinite pursuit of security, or it can inspire you to walk the longest, highest, and most gorgeous line possible—right here, right now, while those feet still work and those hips still shake.

THE QUESTION OF CHILDREN

FEW THINGS ALTER the balance of time, money, and purpose more than the decision to start a family.

I long imagined that I might have kids in my mid-30s. But as that moment approached, I found myself happily engaged with my work, friends, travels, writing, dancing, and other adventures. Nor was I part of (or seriously seeking) a long-term relationship. So I kicked the can down the road and waited for the "right person" or "right situation" to arise.

This delusion persisted until age 41: the same moment that, were I to have a womb, emergency sirens would be blaring. That's when I sat down, leveled with myself, and recorded all of my hesitations, assumptions, and fears about parenting in a post entitled *Conflicted Thoughts About Having Kids.*

What this exercise revealed was, above all else, that I fear becoming a zombie. I fear losing the spark that ignites me as a writer, traveler, and educator. I fear the financial obligations inherent in providing a so-called "normal" childhood. I fear becoming an overworked and underslept curmudgeon, slowly drowning in the treacherous waters of modern parenting culture, exhausted by the daily demands of domestic servitude, stewing in regret about the expansive life I left behind—all of which might make me a pretty bad dad.

How ironic. The guy who spent two decades working alongside

families with alternative, adventurous, and self-directed lives can't envision one for himself.

I've met families who backpack and bike-tour with their kids, families who live on boats, and families who live abroad. Dirtbag rich families *do* exist. They often pursue a scaled-down version of the dirtbag rich dream—one that offers more financial security and geographic stability, especially when children are young—but it can be done. You're unlikely to enjoy the same time wealth and financial ease that you did in your pre-parent days, but your life will be filled with a new and profound well of purpose, one that will hopefully persist until your dying days.

Some people clearly and unequivocally want children, and they'll do whatever it takes to make this happen. If this is you, my hat is off. Child-rearing is a rodeo, and simply staying in the saddle is a worthy challenge. Thank you for perpetuating the species, and have fun with those little rippers.

Some people clearly and unequivocally do *not* want children, and prefer to spend their time around other adults, doing adult stuff. If this is you, then you're primed to live your wildest dirtbag rich dreams. Go hike all the trails, paddle all the rivers, ski all the mountains, and visit all the countries!

And then there are those like me—and perhaps like you—who cherish their adult lives, feel deeply hesitant about the trade-offs involved in modern parenting, yet still crave the purpose offered by relating deeply to young people. Is there space for us in the world?

COOL AUNTS, UNCONVENTIONAL EDUCATORS, AND CRAZY GUYS ON BIKES

WHETHER YOU ACTIVELY decide that you're not a good candidate for child-rearing, you end up partnered with someone who doesn't want (or can't have) kids, or you simply end up running down the clock, you can still live dirtbag rich *and* have meaningful relations with young people.

First, you can become an extremely cool aunt or uncle.

Growing up, I enjoyed a close relationship with an aunt who helped me glimpse life outside the family bubble. Aunt Wendy was (and is) a perpetual bachelorette, a fiercely independent desert rat, an iconoclastic conspiracy theorist, and a kind-hearted humanitarian. When I was a young child, she lived with us for a year to support my mom after my mom's divorce. After that I saw her just once or twice a year, but I looked forward to every encounter—and not just because she bought me Pop-Tarts and video games. In my early twenties, she saw me off on my Pacific Crest Trail adventure, and when I was stuck in my cycle of quitting and fleeing, she welcomed me into her home near Seattle for a spell. I adored hearing her wild stories about becoming a teenage runaway, a van-dwelling hippie in Mexico, and a glass-ceiling-busting corporate executive in the transportation sector. I appreciated her interest in my intellectual development, the bold way she asked personal questions, and how she debated politics without ever taking things personally. Wendy showed me how aunts, uncles, cousins, godparents, and other extended family can matter deeply to young people—and how such roles are fully compatible with a freewheeling, "drop into your life, make memories, disappear again, and check-in with text messages" mode of existence.

Second, you can become an educator. And there are all sorts of ways to "educate," especially when you don't have your own kids.

Life in a nuclear family can be suffocating, no matter how amazing the parents. That's why kids need a swarm of non-parental adults in their lives: mentors, coaches, teachers, tutors, guides, and neighbors. Some educators do their jobs and can still go home to their own kids (or not), like swim coaches, schoolteachers, and art instructors. Then there are the roles suited for childfree adults with specialized skills and high flexibility: roles like summer camp counselor, international trip leader, wilderness backpacking guide, international language teacher, boarding school houseparent, high-level sports coach, and residential therapeutic counselor. (Even if you never formally work in education, you can take your friends' kids on a week-long adventure.) Such positions allow you to work intensively with young people over more extended periods, bringing about profound changes that parents genuinely cannot. And since you know that you'll return to your chilled-out, high-autonomy existence soon enough, you have more energy to give to the young people in your charge.

Finally, kids—and adults, and entire societies—need to see weird, provocative, and adventurous people out there on the road.

To me, this is symbolized by the *crazy guy on a bike*: those mystical voyagers I spy through car windows, pedaling along rural roads and state highways with four fully-loaded panniers, headed to destinations unknown. These "crazy guys" (who are more often than not men) represent some kind of ultimate freedom to me—as do hitchhikers, crust punks, thru-hikers, and other hobo-like figures who don't appear truly destitute. As long as they're not scamming or harming anyone, I've come to believe these world-wanderers are doing the world a genuine service.

I think of my old college friend, Jeff. Always soft-spoken, kind-hearted, and idealistic, Jeff initially tried serving the world by getting a Ph.D. in economics and working in the field of international development. Then he sat multiple 10-day silent meditation retreats, went deep into Buddhism, and decided to radically change his approach. Now his name is Guṇavīro, and he has chosen the life of a wandering monk: walking between cities and towns (in both the US and developing countries like Brazil), begging for food, meditating for hours, and sleeping wherever space is offered (or camping when no such space appears).

Guṇavīro's mission is to vividly experience—and to discuss with anyone who seems genuinely interested—the Buddhist notion of non-attachment. Whereas Jeff once held conventional beliefs about "making an impact" and "contributing to the social good," Guṇavīro now lives his values completely, as he told me over email:

> I have this belief that people need an example more than they need an explanation. I think people are asking themselves who they want to be like, and trying to model themselves on those people. It is rare that just explaining an ideal gets people to reorient their whole lives. But when they see someone with a sense of peace, inner strength, unshakability, balanced compassion, or freedom, then somewhere deep inside, they know *that* is something worth striving for.

Without going so extreme, you can do something similar.

By living dirtbag rich—or even just dirtbag—your wild life, bold choices, and sense of self-authorization can inspire others to do something similar.

Are the *crazy ladies* and *crazy guys on bikes* aware of their impact? Unlikely. And if they are, they must guard against this awareness becoming self-serving or self-glorifying. But I do believe their contribution is real. Like Guṇavīro, they are living their values in public. (This can be done online, too, but real-life interactions always stick better.)

When you enjoy children, it can be hard to commit to being the cool aunt, unconventional educator, or crazy guy on a bike. Families are meaningful projects. Your parents want grandkids. And your biology certainly nudges you toward reproduction, overtly and covertly. (A note I once wrote to myself, "my genes make me want to have babies with you," serves as a mantra-like incantation against my tendency toward overly rapid romantic infatuation.)

Riding the Camino de Santiago in a shark costume, 2022

But instead of fretting about having kids—a choice that my biology allows me to consider for quite a while longer—maybe I should embrace the signs that the world is sending me. Once, before a talk I gave to homeschool parents, the organizer introduced me as someone who "basically has no home and just works for our kids to experience life outside the box, moving from amazing place to even more amazing place with kids in tow." More recently, a European dance friend told me, "Of course you won't have kids, Blake. Your ideas are the seeds that you're spreading across the world."

In short, by electing *not* to start your own family and leaning fully into your role as a family member, educator, or crazy x on a y, you can still play a fantastically fun and important role in the lives of children.

Like Guṇavīro, you can show the world your peace, inner strength, compassion, and freedom—as well as your glorious weirdness, enthusiasm, creativity, and aliveness.

How you do this, and with whom, is up to you.

MODERATELY PRIVILEGED AND HIGHLY IDEALISTIC

THE MOMENT I began championing unschooling, alternative schools, and other forms of innovative, consent-based education, I started hearing: *But not everyone can do this!* Not everyone can afford to have one parent at home. Not everyone can support a child's self-directed learning. Not everyone can attend a private school, even a highly subsidized one. *Instead of abandoning public education, let's work hard to improve it! Until we're all free, no one is free!*

Well-intentioned—and misguided.

Public schools have faced the same kinds of problems and critiques since their inception. Classes are too big. Students are unmotivated. Teachers are underpaid. The "wrong" subjects are emphasized. Grades don't mean much. The system favors the wealthy.

We like to believe that schools can level the playing field between people of all backgrounds. But even if you offer full-ride scholarships to top private schools or widen access to the most innovative public schools, students still bring powerful inequalities from their homes, upbringings, and accidents of birth.

Helping everyone to become "free" turns out to be rather tricky, and waiting for this miracle before permitting any radically different approaches is a sure-fire way to preserve the status quo.

Improving education isn't an "either/or" proposition. When some people step outside the system and tinker with alternatives, they pave the way for others. Like the proverbial *crazy guy on a bike*, unschoolers can inspire homeschoolers, and alternative schools can inspire conventional schools. We need an ecosystem, not a monoculture. Not everyone can do this, and that's okay.

If you're one of the lucky few who can take a different path through school or work, here's the thing: you need to do your thing publicly. Be an open book. Make it easy for others to learn from you.

There's an old distinction between two schools of Buddhism: Theravada, which focuses on personal salvation, and Mahayana, which aims for the enlightenment of all beings. I'm saying: take the Mahayana approach. Go discover your secrets, but don't hoard them. Come back and share with the rest of us.

The same goes for dirtbag rich. Not everyone can figure out a way to earn good money in little time. Not everyone can find housing that's both safe and affordable. Not everyone enjoys a reliably healthy body, zero student debt, or economically independent family members.

This shouldn't stop you from trying.

The classic work-life deal is this: earn as much money as you can now, without much concern for time or purpose, in the hope that you'll enjoy plenty of time, purpose, and money in retirement.

The dirtbag rich deal is this: Try to have it all now—deep purpose, spacious time, and sufficient money—at the risk of having less money, and perhaps more problems, later in life.

If you fail badly in your dirtbag rich ambitions, you may end up relying on family, government, or a romantic partner. You may live in a trailer, work at a big box store, or face daily indignities that more diligent adults—those who *sucked it up* and *did what they must*—consider humiliating.

The risks are real. The dirtbag rich deal is not for everyone.

Much like alternative education, attempting to live dirtbag rich is best suited for a certain group: the moderately privileged and highly idealistic.

"Moderately privileged" means that you, like me, were born into a country of relative wealth and freedom. It means that you've enjoyed good health, a stable upbringing, a decent education, and membership in a society that doesn't strongly discriminate against you. (For my social-justice-oriented readers: this demographic may be larger than you imagine.)

"Highly idealistic" means that you, like me, are not content to merely reproduce your privilege. It means you prefer to redistribute your unearned gifts by living a different kind of life, and sharing what you learn with others: a guinea pig for social change.

Rather than dwelling in ease and comfort, you will risk your future security in the name of bridging cultures, building movements, innovating with business, and tinkering with new notions of "progress" and "freedom." Instead of accruing riches only for your genetic lineage, you will attempt to make a unique and purposeful contribution to a much wider circle: Team Human.

Rather than aiming for an early retirement, you will aim to continue working and serving—today, tomorrow, and maybe all the way to your dying days—while not working *so* hard that you burn yourself out and become of little use to anyone.

Not everyone can do this. But there are many "moderately privileged" people who can afford to become a bit more idealistic, and many with less privilege who nevertheless possess the idealism, fearlessness, and spirit of adventure necessary to live this way.

The most important question isn't: *Can everyone in the world become dirtbag rich today?* It's: *Will you do more good, both for yourself and others, by trying to live differently?*

NUTS AND BOLTS

WHAT MORE CAN I say? Go brush your teeth and read a few good books about entrepreneurship. Spend less than you earn, year after year. Make friends and keep promises. Move your body every day, in such a way that you can keep moving it tomorrow. Avoid buying a fancy mattress for as long as possible. Abandon your current life path in a dramatic fashion at least once, but probably no more than three times. Eat things with short shelf lives. Quit smoking. (Sitting is smoking, and infinite-scroll is smoking.) Sleep on strangers' floors. Take partner dance classes. Learn how to cook five basic, excellent meals from cheap, universal ingredients. Email that person who really wants to help you do your own thing, and say, "Please help me do my own thing!" Share publicly about what you're up to, no matter how niche the topic or limited the audience. Fix little problems with your car or bike before they become big problems. Swim in a questionable body of water every now and then. Hand-write a few love letters. Walk across x, where x is a city, country, or entire mountain range. Stop asking young people what they want to be when they grow up and start asking what they want to feel. And if you're waking up sick to your stomach about where you must go and what you must do each day—stop.

That's all I know. I'm in the middle of this journey, too. If you want to see where it's taken me, visit blakeboles.com. I promise to keep reporting from the trenches.

The adventurer Tom Allen once explained how to cycle around the world in three easy steps:

1. Get a bicycle. It doesn't matter too much which one, as long as it's comfortable, but you won't get far without it.
2. Quit your job. You'll need a few years for a lap of the planet, so write to your boss explaining that you're sorry but there's something you have to do. (Skip this step if you are a student/unemployed/retired.)
3. Start. You can't cycle around the world without starting. So strap your stuff to your bike, ask your neighbor to look after the dog/cat/goldfish, and pedal away from home.

Once you have accomplished the above three steps, the rest will work itself out.

You *could* take a few other steps, Tom continued, like 4) do research, 5) get fit, 6) save money, 7) buy equipment, 8) plan a route, 9) share it all on social media, 10) get sponsorship, 11) ride for a cause, 12) get media coverage, 13) burn your bridges, 14) break a record, 15) gather data, or 16) set goals. But each new step adds complexity, lowering the chance that you'll get rolling in the first place.

Tom's right: the hardest part is starting.

You don't necessarily need to quit your job to start. Nor does starting commit you to living some wildly alternative life, forever and ever.

But there's almost certainly a step you need to take on your way to whichever version of "dirtbag rich" is yours. Maybe it's a hard conversation, a long-postponed adventure, or a radical experiment.

No matter the step, it will feel like a lungful of mountain air before jumping into a frigid lake, the first glimpse of a foreign city as you descend through the clouds, or the warm embrace of a kind stranger welcoming you into their home.

Put the book down, and take the step.

ACKNOWLEDGMENTS

BIG THANKS TO all the *Dirtbag Rich* interviewees. Even if your name doesn't appear in the book, your spirit does.

Much of this book was first written in my newsletter, "The Adventures of Blake," between 2022-2025. Thanks to all who commented publicly and privately on those pieces. If you're hungry for backstory, go mine the archives.

Alan Burnce and Olson Pook edited my chicken scratches into something of substance. Chris, Jonathan, Meagan, Anne, Rachel, Mary Ann, and Carolee helpfully commented on an early draft. The phrase "dirtbag rich" was coined by Tim Mathis, who generously supported my adopting it. Brendan Leonard helped immensely with recruiting interview subjects and illustrating the book in his delightful, signature style.

Paul Millerd's quote is from his book, *Good Work*. Verlyn Klinkenborg's quote is from his book, *Several Short Sentences About Writing*. The phrase "crazy guy on a bike" is borrowed from Neil Gunton's website of the same name. Tom Allen's quote is from his article, "How To Cycle Round The World In 3 Easy Steps." The "Dancing fusion in Europe" photograph is taken by Maria Mizgalo. And the author photograph is by Maria Kravchik.

No AI was used in writing *Dirtbag Rich*.

ABOUT THE AUTHOR

BLAKE BOLES is a traveling writer, experiential educator, and partner dancer.

His previous books include *Why Are You Still Sending Your Kids to School?*, *The Art of Self-Directed Learning*, *Better Than College*, and *College Without High School*.

Learn more at blakeboles.com.

www.ingramcontent.com/pod-product-compliance
Lightning Source LLC
LaVergne TN
LVHW011714060526
838200LV00051B/2902